Other Titles by Marc Beaudin

Voices. Elevated.: 10 Years of the Elk River Writers Workshop. (editor) WordFire Press, 2025

Poet to Poet: Elk River 30 for 30 Poetry Prompt Collection. (editor) WordFire Press, 2025

The Sky Too Is Concrete. CrowVoice Audio, 2025. Spoken word featuring music by Mike Johnston and Mike Gilmore

These Creatures of a Day. FootHills Publishing, 2024. Poetry

From Coltrane to Coal Train: An Eco-Jazz Suite. CrowVoice Audio, 2022. Spoken word featuring music by Dana Colley, Billy Conway and Laurie Sargent

Life List: Poems. Riverfeet Press, 2020. Poetry & birds, with monotypes by Storrs Bishop

Vagabond Song: Neo-Haibun from the Peregrine Journals. Elk River Books, 2015

The Moon Cracks Open: A Field Guide to the Birds & Other Poems. Heal the Earth Press, 2008

MORE ACCLAIM FOR *VAGABOND SONG*

"A poet's song to the rewards of wandering and the joy of the highway. It's a bracing tonic and one this sorry, sad-assed, gadget-obsessed nation needs to hear again and again."
    –**William Hjortsberg**, author of *Jubilee Hitchhiker: The Life and Times of Richard Brautigan* and *Falling Angel*

"A love song to the open road, a jazzy, freewheeling hitchhiking memoir ... a rollicking road trip into the beating heart of the Eternal Now. Hop in and enjoy the ride."
    –*Montana Quarterly*

"Here is a poet's road trip, as drunk on travel as Bashō, tracing the blue highways with a dazzling prose. We should all take strength from his impressive traverse."
    –**Doug Peacock**, author of *Grizzly Years* and *Was It Worth It?: A Wilderness Warrior's Long Trail Home*

"In *Vagabond Song*, Beaudin recounts two decades of life on the road, from the uncertainties of his first hitchhiking experience through the many adventures of his seeker's journey. Beaudin intertwines expansive and lyric passages as he weaves his personal narrative, and he has plenty to say about history and politics, about religion, mythology and the spiritual curiosity that drives him."
    –**Tami Haaland**, former Montana poet laureate and author of *If I Had Said Beauty*

"Blending the genres of memoir, travel and poetry, *Vagabond Song* unfolds like an impressionistic series of trip logs. The work is as ambitious as it is fluid. ... Beaudin hits the road seeking a poetry of freedom & wilderness, both physical & psychic, by confronting the ravages of history, religion and greed, along with his own fears and hypocrisies while incessantly seeking lessons to be learned in the wild expansive spaces of earth and mind."
    –*The Review Magazine*

"*Vagabond Song* is a book that may change the reader, deepen understanding, remain with one—a *vade mecum* of the soul—long after one has read it. The book leaves one hungry for more books by this author."
                             —*Hollywood Progressive*

"This is a volume you can dig into and find treasure."
                             —*Big Sky Journal*

"What a roadsong! No matter where I opened the book, I was drawn into the bright moment of the journey. Only a poet could fashion such a book."
         —**Tamarack Song**, author of *Journey to the Ancestral Self* and director of Teaching Drum Outdoor School

"Is this an open-road memoir from 50 or 60 years ago, or from tomorrow? Both, one suspects. Beaudin has been some places and seen some things. I'm not sure when he slept or what exactly he does for a profession, as opposed to a living, but it's an entertaining read. This is the kind of book parents will hide from their graduating children, but which will be found nonetheless."
               —**Rick Bass**, author of *With Every Great Breath*

"Such a damn good read it was impossible to put down once begun and then left me enraged because when it was finished it was finished. Wanted more. Lots more. … Simply put, Beaudin is a SUPERB writer and storyteller."
                             —*Arts Saginaw*

"Thumbs up."
    —*Foreword Reviews*

"Beaudin's sensibility is that of a companion, an observer of the world, a Virgil on Blue Highways. When I stopped to rest, I heard his typewriter clicking and clacking in my head. *Vagabond Song* is one of those books that you're never truly done with."
            —**Andrew Guschausky, Cassiopeia Books**

Portrait of the author, circa 1992
created with black paper & an X-Acto knife
by fellow traveler John Francis Bueche

VAGABOND SONG

"*Sozorogami no mano ni tzukite kokoro wu kuruwase,
Dōsojin no maneki ni aite.*"
—Matsuo Bashō
The Narrow Road to the Deep North

"The gods of wanderlust take possession of me,
The spirit-guardians of the road beckon me on."
—author's poor translation

Neo-Haibun from the Peregrine Journals

10th Anniversary Edition – Revised & Expanded

by
MARC BEAUDIN

Artwork by
EDD ENDERS

2025
Elk River Books
Livingston, Montana

Copyright © 2015, 2025 by Marc Beaudin
All artwork copyright © 2015, 2025 by Edd Enders

All rights reserved. No part of this book may be reproduced or transmitted in any form or by any means without the written consent of the publisher.

No generative artificial intelligence (AI) was used in the writing or design of this work. The author and publisher **expressly prohibit** any entity from using this publication for purposes of training AI technologies to generate text or images, including, without limitation, technologies that are capable of generating works in the same style or genre as this publication.

Revised edition.

Published by Elk River Books, LLP
PO Box 2212
Livingston, MT 59047
ElkRiverBooks.com
press@elkriverbooks.com

International Standard Book Number: 978-0-9863040-6-4

Cover: "Swingly Road" by Edd Enders, eddendersart.com

for my brother:
Brian (Mato) Aimesbury
and
for my ponies:
Gus, Hero, Clyde, Bashō, Otto & Buck Mulligan

"I dream of journeys repeatedly …"
—Theodore Roethke

Contents:

Preface to the 10th Anniversary Edition xiii
Foreword by William Heyen xv

prelude 1
M-72 (*first movement*) 3
interlude 13
Trail Ridge & West Elk Loop (*second movement*) 15
caesura: Loon Point Camp 57
State Rd. 107 & the Music Highway (*third movement*) 61
interlude 79
M-46 (*fourth movement*) 81
interlude 95
The Chicken Bus Highway, Part I (*fifth movement*) 97
interludio 121
The Chicken Bus Highway, Part II (*sixth movement*) 123
caesura: Symposia 153
A1 & the Wicklow Way (*seventh movement*) 157
caesura: Squatemala 177
Highway 2 (*eighth movement*) 181
interlude 195
Flying Cloud to the Warrior Trail (*ninth movement*) 197
interlude 225
Coastal Highway (*second movement, reprise*) 227
coda: The Grizfork 243

Bonus Tracks

Casa Parota 247
interlude 251
The Hundred Highways Tour 253

Bios 285
Sources 286

Preface

MY ARCHEOLOGICAL DIG CONTINUES, ten years later. When I first wrote *Vagabond Song*, I was excavating old journals going back to the very beginning of my road trip days, over 20 years in my past then, over 30 now. Piecing together the episodes from scraps of memory, nearly indecipherable scribblings and the poems salvaged from that era. Remembering the wonder and freshness of it all. Marveling over that young kid who discovered for himself the magic of "free travel" – setting out on the road with no agenda, no plans, no destination and allowing the world to unfold itself as it willed.

This new edition features two new "bonus tracks" – "Casa Parota," a haibun from a recent trip to a small, roadless village in Jalisco, Mexico, and "The Hundred Highways Tour," a condensed version of the trip logs from the tour for the original release. Most of the movements, especially the poems, have been revised (or as I teach my workshop participants, *re-listened* – getting closer, I hope, to the intrinsic music of the poem and trusting the music to take the poem where it needs to go). This edition also adds eight new illustrations by the fantastic artist Edd Enders.

Speaking of Edd, I'd like to thank him for adding his incredible work to this project – it's the perfect complement. Thanks also to Lisa Snow who traveled with me for most of the 100 Highways Tour, and to the generous and welcoming people at all the venues who hosted me. I'd also like the thank the editors of the journals where many of these poems first appeared: *Avocet, Cardinal Sins, Fragile Arts Quarterly, GlassFire, Haiku Journal, Outsider Writers, Shot Glass Journal, Talking Earth Anthology* and *Watershed*, as well as the publishers who put out my books where some of the poems also appear: M.L. Liebler at Ridgeway Press, Dan Rice at Riverfeet Press and Michael and Carolyn Czarnecki at FootHills Publishing.

    A lot has changed in these past ten years. This country that I've traveled, that I've called home (whatever that means), has sunk into a dark and ugly morass of hate, fear and outright fascism, led by a criminal buffoon and his nationalist cult members. Attacks on the freedoms and diversity this book celebrates are at an all-time high. But so too is our resistance. The guerilla poets who not only speak truth to power, but beauty as well, will not and cannot be silenced. Democracy is in the libraries, the bookshops, the galleries, the music halls, the theatres, the forests, the mountains, and most of all, forever and always, in the streets.

    This book is full of Vagabond Angels, arriving at just the right moment to set me off on the next *wonder-full* leg of the journey. I remember decades ago when I saw Kurt Vonnegut speak, and he defined an angel as a decent person in an indecent world. And then he told us to be angels. We need that call now more than ever. Thanks for traveling with me, and thanks for being an angel.

–Marc

Foreword

FOLKS, IT HAS BEEN MY GOOD FORTUNE to have known many "feral" (a favorite Marc Beaudin word & concept) saintly singer-travelers & trans-spatial seers – Allen Ginsberg & Antler & Edwina Seaver & Al Hellus & Anthony Piccione come to mind – but the author of *Vagabond Song* (note the singular, the Oneness of so many highway melodies & dissonances) is a cat in his own category of howl & highway hymn. It's our luck that he's made a book from his old journals/marginalia/memory albums, one that will persist in our minds as a classic companion of blue moonways & on-the-road travels with Charlie.

In one of the remarkable poems that distills experience here, Beaudin dreams of tourist cadavers who have ice picks in their ears, who "would begin to sing, but, / deafened by the picks, / would never hear their song." After this nightmare of deafness, the poet sinks in illness on an outhouse floor & waits "to be purified." This is this book's quest, the human desire for purification, the desire for us to be able to be not tourists but true living travelers, always within the mystery of home, who can sing & can hear our own songs.

Vagabond Song is a wonder of conscience & stamina, of poetry, as Beaudin enters the divine circulation, & we with him, by "thumb power" & soul-power, to Chicago & Copán & San Fran & back around by way of Europe & bison & totem herons as he moves toward the great mystery in this his/our achieved Tao written as though with one inhalation-exaltation by one of our beatific angels along the trail.

–William Heyen

prelude

Not much is known about Miscellaneous Jones
He walked a lot of roads
but always wiped the dust from his boots
He was partial to rhubarb pie & drank his coffee black
He did most of his talking with his eyes
but if you heard his voice, even once,
you'd never quite be able
to shake it

M-72
first movement

IF I DON'T GET BACK ON THE ROAD I'm going to lose my dog-damn mind howling mad and barking crazy like some burning saint. Give us this night our vagrant moon. Give us this day a double yellow line flashing like a beacon of endless possibility. Give us the music unfurling like multi-colored prayer flags across a murmuration sky. Kinetophilia. Go.

Sitting at a gimp-legged table, kinetophobic fingers hovering over silent keys, my reflection in the frosted window refuses to make eye contact. I thought this would work. I thought this was just what I needed. To hole up in a borrowed cabin, build a fire against the coming winter and writewritewrite.

The romance of it. The poetry: The writer in a lover's cabin in the Michigan Northwoods. Cupboards stocked with pasta and wine. He writes all day, late into the night. A single Coltrane tape to fill the air. He plays the clacking keys of his Remington in syncopated unity with that prophetic, wall-crashing horn. The pages fill with the black dance of words. On weekends the lover arrives with more wine and all the delicious aromas of life and lust and laughter. Lying in bed, they read the fresh pages. They read the topography of their bodies. They read the words of fire and granite. They read the poetry of hair and skin, flesh and sweat. She goes back to the city and he goes back to the typewriter. Everything flows smooth and luminous. The pages become the book. The book is good and strong and speaks the words that need speaking.

That was the plan. ... Mice and men, boys. Mice and men.

After nearly three months, I have maybe a half-dozen pages. Her visits grow less frequent, less poetic.

The cabin becomes a prison, my typewriter a cellmate. Moonstar, this hand-me-down Remington Streamliner, is a worthy companion, but after all this time alone together we have very little to say to one another. A blank page has been staring back at me for days now. *All mine Oten reedes bene rent and wore and my poor Muse* has split for downtown, waiting in line with the other plasma prostitutes. Short walks in the pine-crazed air aren't enough – I need miles to burn and voices not my own in my head. I need change that comes faster than the change of light slanting across the ghosts of blueberry bushes and withered stalks of mullein as the autumn drifts into winter.

It's something about measuring life by the clicking of miles rather than the ticking of a clock. Some necessity for motion. Bashō attributes it to *Dōsojin*, literally "road ancestor deity." The Dōsojin are guardian spirits of the road. They beckoned to Bashō throughout his life. They are comrades of Miscellaneous Jones, dance partners of Zorba Chaos, children of Moses Om. And now they are knocking at my door. I need to move.

So, with my army-surplus pack loaded with a change of clothes, rain poncho, railroad gloves, wool blanket, sleeping hat, plastic tarp, a battered copy of the Upanishads, an even more battered road atlas, journal, smooth-flowing pen, sheath knife, Ohio Blue Tips in a waterproof vial, roll of duct tape, mess kit, toothbrush, jug of water, block of cheese, bag of orzo, nuts, raisins and two apples, I walk the mile of dirt road to Highway 72 west of Grayling, birthplace of Jim Harrison, who wrote, "God is terse. The earth's proper scripture could be carried on a three-by-five card if we weren't drunk on our own blood," and a page later, "I poke my stick in the moon's watery face, then apologize."

At the side of the road I drop my pack to the gravel, letting it rest against my leg. I cast my thumb into the waters of the highway. Sometimes my hitchhiking is akin to fly-fishing: dancing my thumb into the ripples of oncoming traffic, luring the drivers into the adventure of picking up this longhaired, bearded stranger in torn jeans, secondhand M-65 jacket, duct-taped boots and a dead man's hat. I guide their cars to the shoulder, reeling them in so gently they don't even realize they're hooked. … But this morning I'm in the mood for lazy old worm-fishing: thumb slung low – red-and-white bobber floating on a sleeping lake with a worm drooping on a hook below.

The sun is breaking free of the tree line and the air murmurs stories of wood smoke and diesel. A deer-crossing sign riddled with bullet holes stands next to me, our shadows wavering into dust-coated weeds.

As Miscellaneous Jones says, "A weed is just a flower nobody wants."

The road is lined with chicory, Queen Anne's lace, burdock and clover – all edible, all beautiful, all healthy. All unwanted.

Vagabond Song

> Garden of roadside weeds
> breathing me as I breathe them
> Greeting the sun with slight bows
> & nods & remembering
> refusing to forget:
> Eden hasn't gone anywhere

    Seven cars, three semis, two RVs and a motorcycle pass. The biker, as always, gives me an encouraging thumbs-up and my own thumb spins quickly into a peace sign, then back. The car drivers try to avoid eye contact, pretending to study something interesting on the far side of the road. The RVers glare suspiciously. A mile later, they will notice the sign: "Prison Area – Do Not Pick Up Hitchhikers" and have all their stereotypes confirmed. America, Inc. loves to instill fear in its sheeple. Give them fear and they will buy anything that promises security, whether cell phones, spy drones or war. Sex may sell, but fear creates lifetime customers.
    Then a pickup picks me up. Such well-named vehicles.
    The driver, mid-sixties, leaner than he seems used to, flips open the small cooler on the seat between us as he pulls back onto the road and eases up to speed.
    "Wanna beer?"
    I pull out a cold one and crack it. He drains his and tosses it behind the seat, so I hand mine to him and crack another.
    We race between gray-green walls of jack pine cut now and then by a yellow blaze of poplar. The sky warms to the idea of another blue day, one of the last before winter seals a concrete vault over us all. We drink our beers and feel out how much talking either of us wants to do. Some rides are all questions: Where ya headed? Where ya comin' from? How long ya been at it? Others ask nothing, but just talk away like they've had it all bottled up for

miles and the presence of another set of ears breaks the dam. Life stories and memory lanes, elusive dreams and big plans. This guy, though, is a puzzle. He'll ask a question but doesn't seem to hear the answer, as if he'd never asked anything in the first place. My questions are met with silence, broken eventually by not so much an answer as a response to something deep within that perhaps my question has roused.

"Do you know what creek that was?" gets a long pause, followed by: "I retired up here from Detroit. Thought to do a lot of fishing with the wife. She loved to catch a trout or largemouth. Used to have a little outboard, but sold that with the rest of it."

I wonder if I should ask the thousand questions his story raises, but there's a quality of trepidation in the silence that follows. I wait for him to continue. We finish our beers and start new ones.

By the time he drops me at the fork of I-75 and I-27, I'm floating delicately in my own little boat of inebriation. The birches and aspens along the roadsides dance in rolling waves and from somewhere a crow calls out its graveled song.

But the fork of two expressways, with massive hulks of metal hurtling by at undogly speeds, is not the place for delicate floating.

Rapids ahead. Time to switch to fly fishing.

I pick out a blue sedan, raise my thumb high and snap, rolling my line into an invisible eddy that will bring our separate journeys briefly into one. We will both be changed forever, but that's true for every encounter. Every connection, even just a moment of eye contact, changes us. Streams merge and diverge. Waters mix. Which droplet is you and which is me?

Three rides, 106 miles and I'm walking Saginaw, birthplace of

Vagabond Song

Theodore Roethke, who wrote, "When I breathe with the birds, the spirit of wrath becomes the spirit of blessing, and the dead begin from their dark to sing in my sleep."

The brick walls of this town are tired of holding up windows that have lost their light. The river is lethargic enough that at times, with the right wind, it flows backwards.

>   Walking the streets in a dead man's hat
>   & all his dreams & memories are still inside
>   The walls are tattooed with faded names
>   & I button up my coat & try to hide

The history of a place is never history. It's here now, always.

1819. General Lewis Cass places five barrels of whiskey in front of several Ojibwa and Odawa chiefs who, with the help of Louis Campau the local trader, have already been made, strategically, into alcoholics. Cass tells them they can't have the whiskey until they sign his paper. Six million acres for $1,000 annually, to be paid in silver. Six million acres of generational maple-sugaring grounds, wild-ricing lakes, vast gardens of the "Three Sisters" of corn, beans and squash. Forest cornucopias of game, herbs, fruits, nuts, medicine and manufacturing materials like birch, basswood, nettle and cedar. Hundreds of rivers and lakes teeming with fish. Graves of unnumbered ancestors. Six million squares of Home for a handful of silver ... and that whiskey, just out of reach – the one thing that can douse the raging fires in their heads.

Cass and Campau know there is one chief, Kiskawko, who will never sign, so he is given enough whiskey ahead of time to keep him away from the proceedings. "Chief" is a loaded word. It doesn't mean what the U.S. government and the history books say it does. They pretend it's equivalent to king or president or some other term to describe an autocrat with coercive power over others. Someone who could bind all his people into a treaty agreement with another sovereign. But that kind of antidemocratic tyranny is as foreign to the minds and bodies of the Anishinaabe as that whiskey calling to them from inside those barrels, and just as deadly. Traditionally, the dodem or clan system ensures that hereditary clan leaders pursue the will of their clan and serve the tribe in matters of their particular clan's specialty: Bear clan for health and security, Eagle for education, Turtle for justice, etc. But there is no one who has absolute authority over the rest: all important decisions require agreement from each and every clan. Which is why a man named Ausawamic believes the treaty is nothing but paper, and a handful of silver can never replace his homeland. Each year, when the government agent comes to Saginaw to disburse the annuity, Ausawamic takes his payment, walks to the bank of the river and throws the coins into the depths.

Okemos and Owasso sign the treaty and now have cities named after them. Nobody has heard of Ausawamic. As in all our histories, the true heroes have no monuments.

> Walking the streets in a dead man's hat
> the taste of whiskey on the air
> & all his silver is sinking down
> Ophelia with cornflowers in her hair

I slip into Ewald's, on the bank of Ausawamic's protest, crouched troll-like beneath the Court Street Bridge. Ma's off tonight. Dee is slinging drafts to the pool players and barstool rodeo queens. I'm nearly broke, but Dee's buying. She pours a drink like a rainbow – it would be an insult to all that is luminous to decline. I grab my regular table by the window and pull journal

Vagabond Song

and pen from my pack. A couple of beers to lubricate the gears of poetry. Yes and again yes.

View from My Window at Ewald's

Five concrete pillars
holding the silence of the bridge
The bar across the street –
gaudy face slapped over sallow brick
Nothing in the road, not even
a dead dog

A green dumpster, a red fire hydrant:
the closest I'll get to Christmas this year
Lionel with one glove
looking for empties
A blind light scattering bits of darkness
like breadcrumbs

& in front of everything –
my favorite bartender's reflection
pulling her hair back
& swaying to the song on the jukebox
played with the last of my money

And when the money's gone, the road is the most luxurious home you can afford. Come morning I'll be gone.

I spend the night on a friend's couch after a small reunion of the old gang from Pablo's Fortress. The Fortress was an eastside deliriumscape set of rooms above a bass-thumping liquor store on Jefferson Avenue. Through my college years, a rotating tribe of friends and strangers lived there, crashed there, partied there and explored beyond Blake and Huxley's doors of perception there: almost daily expeditions, via one route or another.

The few of us who are still in touch and still in town gather guitars and cheap wine, pass a few joints and rekindle the madness. In the morning I enjoy a gift of eggs and thick bacon at Tony's then head back out on those welcoming roads following the path of imagined ancestors.

Grandpa Scarecrow

He throws the full moon over his shoulder
& rumbles across the field
like a John Deere tractor
picking bits of tobacco from his lips
arms swaying in unison
with the broad rustling leaves

The crows scream his name like a battle cry
"*Hoka hey*, Scarecrow – today is a good day to die"
But his gray bones
like these dry stalks of corn
will stand their ground for yet another winter

Grandpa Scarecrow toes the asphalt snake
rubs his gold tooth for luck
& conjures a ride with his magic thumb
He settles back, yellowed hands on his knees
as the car fills with the smell of damp straw
"Where ya headed, Grandpa?" I ask

   "Home," he says
   "Always home."

interlude

Miscellaneous Jones sent me a postcard
General Delivery / Grayling, Michigan
I had to hitch into town to get it

It said, "Every tyrant
is a killer of poets.
That should tell us something
about the potential power
of what we do."

And then it said,
"Wish you were here."

There was no return address

Trail Ridge & West Elk Loop
second movement

NEARLY TWO DECADES OF BEING ON THE ROAD has to start somewhere. Long before those days at the cabin with Moonstar. Long before I learned advanced thumb techniques and how to score anything needed (free food, free beds, free beer, free love, freedom). Before I knew this was a vocation rather than a pastime, a way of life – in both the mundane and Taoist senses of the phrase – rather than a diversion. Before I'd read Kerouac or London, before I heard Hank Williams sing, "I love you baby but you got to understand, when the Lord made me he made a ramblin' man." Before all of that, I simply cashed in the change I had moldering away in several old wine jugs and bought a ticket on a westbound bus.

New army-surplus canvas pack stashed belowdecks and a new journal ready to catch the coming music, we slink past the burned-out houses and boarded-up liquor stores of eastside Saginaw, home of Rudy Martinez, aka "?" who sang "You're gonna cry 96 tears." Packs of feral dogs and hookers in thrift-store heels

Vagabond Song

– the only ones on the streets at this hour. Vacant lots of broken glass and the rusted skeletons of industry, but the weeds splintering the sidewalks promise renewal. Someday the gray will give way to green. The Earth will reclaim what is hers and the people will throw away their TVs and Oldsmobiles and walk barefoot through the grasses.

> Wisp of wildflower
> struggling through the concrete
> stops the next footstep

The bus leaves town and closes the door behind it, wheezing and coughing its diesel breath into the iron morning air. Sidewalks give way to irrigation ditches. Fields and woodlots broken intermittently by swaybacked barns and stoic farmhouses. Railyards and rummage sales. Cars on blocks and sheets on clotheslines. Hawk on a utility pole. Old woman checking her empty mailbox. Boots on fence posts. Bloated deer carcass gathering crows. Boy fishing from a one-lane bridge. Cloud of gulls following a tractor across a field of worm-rich mud …

Over the years, there have been many bus trips: cross-country journeys that quickly descend into cruel and unusual punishment, daily runs to the college with the voiceless far-eyed yogi in work boots, chicken buses through volcanic dreams, cross-town rides with born-again zombies drooling about Dog and Jeebus and my need to repent – always a sense of incarceration, the smell of sweat, the ache of fatigue and the desire to be outside, walking or hitching instead.

By the time we get to Chicago, we're all in a bad mood and capable of crime. But it's nothing a few drinks won't fix.

Into the canyons of downtown Chicago, home of Carl Sandburg, who wrote, "You have loved forty women, but you have only one thumb." I eventually find what I'm looking for. A door booby-trapped with brass bells, red Naugahyde stools lining a time-blackened bar, "Crazy" on the juke and a spattering of regulars contemplating want ads and bowls of peanuts.

I find a spot at the bar and order a "scurvy special" – a cheap draft with slices of lemon and lime. The vitamin C in the fruit protects me from that disease common to all wind-blown wanderers: pirates, vagabondaoists, anarcho-hobos, concrete nomads, thumb pilots, asphalt mariners, rail riders, drifters, rogues, gypsies, vianauts and Uncle Jack's dharma bums. The first one goes down quickly, washing the bus ride from my teeth. When the jukebox falls silent, I go over and drop my quarter in. In honor of the city I'm in, I punch up some Muddy Waters, who says, "Don't the highway look lonesome after the sun done gone down?" and then more Patsy, this time "Walkin' After Midnight."

There are three requirements for a perfect bar: pool table, no televisions and Patsy Cline on the jukebox. No pool table here, but other than that, this place has what it takes to get the pen moving.

Walking After Midnight

A crumpled dollar bill
like a distant dripping faucet
my moon is not your moon
& it's time to rename
all the constellations

I have wasted the night
in someone else's dreams
& it seems
I got exactly

Vagabond Song

> what I had coming
>
> I remember the ocean
> swallowing the starlight
> drawing lines on our faces
> then folding like a map
> of all our sorrows
>
> Noah was often seasick
> & wanted nothing more
> than to take a drive in the country
> pale-blue Chevy on a dirt road
> bugs splattering the windshield
> two at a time
>
> At least that's what he told me
> as I poured him another bourbon
> and Patsy Cline poured from the jukebox
> like scotch
>
> But we can never be sure
> of any of our memories
> when the sea is involved

A few more scurvy specials and a bowl of peanuts, then I grab an uptown bus to Milwaukee Avenue – nearly a decade later – for a reading at Myopic Books.

A murder of crows. An unkindness of ravens. A rumba of rattlesnakes. There ought to be a name for a gathering of poets, hunkered into the basement room of the Myopic, armed with three-ring binders loaded with words. During the open mic they get up one by one and pound their heads against the walls, bend the bars off the windows, gnash their teeth and perform all sorts of prestidigitation, exhibitionism and transubstantiation. Then it's my turn.

Trail Ridge & West Elk Loop

>So anyway, I was in the park
>looking for a pigeon to feed

What is this? Did I miss the first part of the story? Is this his introduction? Is this a poem? Who is this guy?

>& this guy comes up to me
>& says, "What are you doing in California?"
>& I say, "I came to watch the sunrise."

I hit 'em hard and fast, never let 'em see it coming. Before they know what's happening, they're soaring with me.

>& he says, "The sun doesn't rise here, it sets."
>& I say, "That's okay,
>I'll just stand on my head."

Is it a poem? I doubt it. But it gets the room. Soon we're all flying together down Highway 1 with the mountains whispering in our left ear, the sea in our right. They laugh and hoot, swoop low when I do, rise as one, roll and dive, and we all land together in a rookery of applause.

A flask is passed around and I launch into another. And another. Now it seems it's not just the room that's with me, but the whole city. When I say the word "thunder," the L train thunders past, shaking our bunker. At "howling dogs," a siren blares by. We pass the flask. I try to stop and they ask for more.

With the exception of books, some junkshop talismans, my typewriter and a box of old letters, everything I own fits in my backpack. I have no job, no bank account, no address. But at this moment of poetry, I'm the richest man in the world.

Vagabond Song

> From the bookstore's basement
> poetry takes hold of this city
> of faceless saints
> & canyons of glass
> & doesn't let go
> until the night runs out
> & a morning train
> pulls loose from its mooring
> whispering, "West."

The rails clack by like a blind man's cane. Tiresias approaching with his inescapable prophecy. Beyond my reflection in the train window, corn and wheat break through the thawing earth. Rusted cars molder into junkyard weeds. Children in torn jeans, with dirty faces, climb a fence and wave sticks, the train becoming a character in their game. Towns appear and fade. Aurora. Davenport. Rock Island. Crossing the Mississippi into the mythological West. Into the ocean of the Great Plains – a sea now littered with islands of concrete. Iowa City. Oskaloosa. Des Moines. Omaha. ... Darkness.

After reading for a while, I click out my overhead light and am suddenly treated to a star-filled sky. I pick out familiar constellations – Scorpius, Cygnus, Aquila ... I make up new ones – Hobo John, Bashō's Walking Stick, Scoot the Three-Legged Cockapoo. Or maybe I only see that last one after falling asleep. Waking and sleeping are almost interchangeable on a night train.

Conrad says, "We live as we dream, alone." But I don't know if he ever took a night train to Colorado. We all dream together, hurtling over the face of the Earth. She spins under us, adding to our speed and weaving our dreams.

The sun eventually sneaks up from behind and slowly overtakes us. The train drifts to a stop and a porter slides open the

Trail Ridge & West Elk Loop

door. I shoulder my pack and step through onto a weathered plank platform smaller than the holding tank at the jail in the twice-misnamed city of Mt. Pleasant, Michigan. Across a field of drowsing grass, a few sun-worn buildings rise from the dust looking vaguely expectant – half-curious to see who's dropped from the train at last. Beyond the buildings, an empty two-lane stretches off in both directions.

They dropped me at the wrong place, I think. I'm supposed to be in Winter Park, a town with a hostel, a grocery, a breakfast joint and at least one good bar. This isn't a town. It's the set for the murder scene of an unmade Hitchcock film.

But then all thought is cut off.

I hadn't been prepared for this. Roaring into a sky close enough to taste, dominating and defining the landscape, performing sleight-of-mind on every thinking creature, changing the pitch and key of the train's song as it pulls away and rumbles through the valley: The Rocky Mountains command attention. I stand there gaping and gawking for long moments trying to remember how to breathe.

> The mountains pull down the sky
> touch it to my lips
> summer & winter are fused
> into one moment of the train's song
> echoing through the valley &
> fading into its own myth

At the first building, beyond on open door labeled "STATION," a man looks up from his ski magazine and greets me with smiling eyes.

"Carl'll be along in a minute," he says.

Apparently my confusion is evident, because he follows with,

Vagabond Song

"He'll give you a lift into town."

"Oh. I was worried this was it."

He laughs and returns to his reading. I sit on a bench outside and drink from my canteen, eager to drain the last of my Chicago water and refill it with the vibrancy of Colorado.

Carl comes and I toss my pack in the bed of his pickup. The door creaks like a hawk mobbed by blackbirds and I slide into the passenger seat. An unlit cigarette hangs from his bottom lip and Loretta Lynn fights her way through the static on the radio. He gives me the "Where ya from? Where ya headin'?" two-step. I give him vague and evasive answers, but not for the sake of being vague and evasive. It's just that the questions hold little meaning for a traveler.

A tourist is from a definite place called "Home" and going to a definite place called "Vacation." But a traveler is home wherever he is. There is no from or to. No past or future. No nouns, only verbs. "Road" is a verb.

I road.

You road.

He/She roads.

We are roading.

Carl drops me at the hostel – a cluster of trailers among flowerbeds and clotheslines. After checking in, I spend the day with short hikes around the outskirts of this dormant ski town, soaking in aromas of spruce and cedar. Thousands of years of humus beneath my feet yield to my weight then push me onward. A trail is unnecessary. The sun-catching evergreens keep the forest floor relatively clear of undergrowth. I'm free to wander – one of the greatest forms of freedom we can know. No lines to follow. No boundaries. No goal.

Trail Ridge & West Elk Loop

A soft whooping, like a thick rope swung in circles, fills the air. I look up as three ravens pass above the forest canopy.

> Raven wind becomes breath
> passing over & through me
> Hey, wake up! Wake up!

My meanderings bring me back to town. I borrow a bike from Polly, who owns the hostel, and make a grocery run: trail mix and cheese, pasta, a can of sauce, bulk oatmeal, peanut butter and a box of crackers. Everything I need for another week on the road.

That night I follow a few other travelers to the local bar. As with most American youth hostels, the guests are primarily European. Travel isn't something valued by Americans. It causes one to see the world less myopically. As Mark Twain says, "Travel is fatal to prejudice, bigotry and narrow-mindedness." But for many Americans, those are strong character traits. If they experience more of the world, beyond the tourist bubble of a resort or guided tour, they might have to accept the overwhelmingly obvious fact that this is not the greatest country in the world. That it is not somehow special, exceptional, blessed by Dog. That borders are drawn to control those within them as much as those without. That all patriotism is a form of fascism. But instead of traveling, our youth are taught to go deep into debt with college loans, ensuring they have to find and keep a job immediately after graduation. Forced to join the ranks of wage-slavery, consume their share of useless crap and come home every night after eight hours of selling their soul, they're too tired to do anything but watch television, which indoctrinates them with the desire for more useless crap. The whole process designed to make certain that the wealth of this Land of the Frisked and Home of the Brayed keeps moving in its proper direction: up.

Which explains why I'm the only American heading to the bar tonight. The others are German, Irish, French and Australian. The talk is politics, spirituality, art, literature and the pathetic state of American beer. We shoot a few games, but none of them are that into pool. So mostly we drink and talk, talk and drink until the bartender is putting up the chairs. The entire walk back, the Irish guy and I try to convince each other which is the best novel ever written. He says *Gatsby* and I say *Ulysses*. Fitting.

A couple days later, I decide to hitch up to the next hostel in my guidebook, a place called Shadowcliff, perched over Grand Lake and offering a trailhead to the Rocky Mountain National Park.

Polly, in her strong and gentle mountain voice, tells me, "Don't wear sunglasses. People need to see your eyes to pick you up."

> Walking to the edge of town
> is stepping to cliff's edge –
> you reach the jumping-off point
> the place for a decision to be made:
> Do I remain who I am or become someone new?
> An unknown bird calls from the tree line
> the wind dances a flock of leaves
> It's time to put the sunglasses away
> & jump

Before this moment, I had clocked thousands of miles by bus and train. I had found rides after a short face-to-face. I had traveled, but always in some prearranged manner.

This is the first moment of stepping onto the road and sticking out my thumb. Anonymous, in the moment, karma-bound hitchhiking – the real deal. I'm nervous about getting picked up. I'm nervous about not getting picked up. I'm not sure where to stand – or whether to stand or walk. I don't know where to hold my thumb. High? Low? Stretched out straight? Tucked in close? Should I smile? Look neutral? Sad and desperate? Pack on or off?

For the first few cars that pass, I do nothing. Just a guy walking down the road. I'm not asking for anything, don't want to impose, content either way, but if you did happen to offer, yeah, sure, a ride would be nice. Thanks.

This method is clearly getting me nowhere. I stop and turn to face the oncoming traffic. After a minute or so, a car comes into view. I take a deep breath and stick out my thumb. The car draws closer. I wait. It dopplers by as if I don't exist – and maybe I don't. It's drafted by a pickup I hadn't noticed, tucked tight behind. I slip the pack from my shoulders and drop it to the roadside. Maybe this is a mistake. Maybe I should go back to town and try to meet someone who's headed this way. Maybe post a sign at the hostel. Nobody picks up hitchhikers anymore. We've had eight long years of Reagan and nearly four of Bush pushing fear and isolation into the national mindset. Random acts of kindness are considered an un-American, commie weakness now. Who am I kidding?

A voice interrupts my thoughts. "Well, ya want a ride or don't ya?"

It's the driver of the pickup. I didn't notice that after he passed, he decided to stop. Must have been the happy-neutral-sad-desperate-confused-nervous look on my face. He had waited for a bit while I was despairing over humanity, then stepped out of the cab and called out.

Vagabond Song

He's about my grandpa's age and reminds me of him in the way he talks. A relaxed and straightforward speech that comes from a long life of hard work close to the land. Humor behind the seriousness, but more seriousness behind that. Every fence row, creek and building holds a memory for him that he unfolds in story after story as we make our way north.

A farm where a girl who brought him apples used to live. A hill where he watched his first fireworks. A road that leads to a town where his brother went to join the war.

At a spattering of time-beaten houses and boarded-up shops, his tone falls.

"Now this here used to be a big mining town. Very prosperous. Ten thousand people."

I look out at the fading buildings. A dog chained to a tree raises its head as we pass. A gray creek trickles through the weeds and rusted heaps of metal.

"What happened?" I ask.

"Company took it all and left."

I scan the expanse and try to imagine it back to life. I'd always pictured ghost towns as movie sets: dust-laden saloons with swinging doors hanging by one hinge, shadows of gunslingers long in the grave lingering just out of sight, stray ball of tumbleweed rolling down the street right on cue. But here is the truth behind the fable: communities drained and discarded by the relentless advance of corporate greed.

Ghost Town

> They dug for the bones of the earth
>   clinging to darkness
> Meanwhile people built homes
> raised kids & corn

> The ore-filled railcars daily rolling east
>   spreading the darkness
> Meanwhile some people died
> some were born
>
> The big shovels scraped – came up empty
>   holding only darkness
> Meanwhile the people stood
> with hands outstretched
>
> Looking for a glimpse of what was promised
>   finding only the darkness
> of yet another
> American dream

At a corner gas station, a sudden cloudburst gets me a quick sympathy ride: newlyweds hiking and camping for their honeymoon. They pass their joy and excitement around the car like a bottle and drop me at the front door of the hostel in Grand Lake. As soon as I check in and stash my gear, I pack my satchel with journal, canteen and trail mix, throw on my druidic rain poncho and hit the trail into Rocky Mountain National Park.

The rain has settled into almost a mist, not so much falling as hovering, lingering between sky and earth, content to be not fully either. Like most of us.

The trail writhes like a serpent, rising and twisting deeper into the spruce and lodgepole forest. The *Bhagavad-Gita* says, "I am Vasuki, god of snakes. I am Ananta, the holy serpent." I rise and fall with Earth-Ananta, feeling its reptilian heartbeat. *Ananta* means "without end, infinite." Like all the best trails.

Its known name is Tonahutu Trail, and eventually it meets and follows Tonahutu Creek and brings me to Granite Falls.

The trail and creek take their name from the Arapaho *Tonal-*

hutu, "Big Meadow," referring to the place still called Big Meadows that stretches out alongside the trail. The Arapaho and Ute used this trail for generations, and before them, unnamed Paleo-Indians lived here. They were the lucky ones – there wasn't yet a Colorado Calvary; there was no Colonel John Chivington to meet them at Sand Creek. His is the face behind the massacre, the finger on the trigger, and may he burn in the Hell that he, as a Methodist preacher, must have vividly imagined.

America is the kind of country where every place echoes with the cries of the slaughtered. Scrape the ground anywhere, and the blood of the dispossessed, the enslaved, the condemned will spill forth. But there is hope to be found in the prophetic words of an Arapaho Ghost Dance song: "*Nanisana, nanisana, nahata bitaawu hanta waa-uhu.* – My children, my children, look! The earth is about to move."

At the waterfall, I perch on a boulder and drain my canteen. Ground squirrels lace over the rocks like pulses of light. An osprey works the shallows above the falls. The water cacophonates over the red and golden rocks glistening in the sunlight that has burned away the last of the rain. "Tonalhutu" dances on my tongue as I close my eyes and listen to the music resonating from every tree and stone.

The Forest

I want to tell you something
about the forest

Snake-dancing light
a memory of ice
moss-cradled rock
every path pathless

> No. I want to tell you nothing
> about the forest

Back at the hostel, I meet a Canadian trustafarian. A rich kid playing the hippie lifestyle before joining Daddy's firm back in Ottawa. Blond curls turbulent, Ethan rolls into the room like a tsunami and talks like a speed-freak. He seems dangerously mad, rabid. He rounds up two British women from the hostel, one of whom he's trying vehemently to make it with, throws me into the mix, and we all pile into his pin-dick sports car and head into town. He buys a case of Heineken and rents a motorboat at the docks. Soon we're blasting around the lake, cutting through our own wake and spilling beer all over ourselves.

The thunderbolts appear, moving fast.

"Looks like a storm coming," I say. "We'd better head in."

Ethan ignores me, laughing wildly as he cuts tighter and faster, careening off walls of water. Lighting flashes in the broiling sky and the thunder is bowling strikes.

"Hey, we can't be out here in lightning. Do you know how dangerous it is?"

"We're fine. Give me another beer!"

I begin to think this guy really is crazy, that he wants to get us all killed. The women plead with him to stop. The man on the shore who rented us the boat is waving his arms and yelling. I consider whether I'll be able to toss the guy overboard if it comes to that. A drastic measure, but if it saves the lives of the rest of us, worth it. He's twice my size – I'm the one who'd end up washed ashore.

A wall of rain races across the lake toward us. The thunder and lightning are hitting simultaneously. Something needs to be done, *now*.

I stand up, bracing myself against a gunwale, and scream at the sky. "Come on, you bastard! This fucking idiot wants to die! Come on, you pathetic little storm, zap this fucker! Zap us all! *Kiiiilll!*"

The pitch of the engine drops and our bow settles back to water level. I turn and look at our captain.

"Jesus, dude!" he says. "You're fucking crazy. I'm taking us in."

I flash a quick smile to the others, but they seem confused over which of us to be more afraid of. We make it to shore and head back to the hostel. The storm passes as quickly as it came, and suddenly the world is new. The air is crisp and scented with ozone and pine. The entire incident seems to dissolve with the last of the clouds and we're in blue-sky moods by the time we arrive.

I overcook pasta for everyone, but we eat the near mush with relish. Halfway through a card game, Ethan, as expected, has drunk himself into a stupor. One of the Brits goes off to bed, urging her friend to do the same. They're leaving early in the morning. But the friend, Shannon, stays up with me. She's the one Ethan has been after, and it pleases me immensely that she didn't fall for his rutting-elk bugling bullshit. We sit out on the deck overlooking the night-whispered forest and share the last beer.

A parenthesis moon rises over the mountains, bleeding through torn rags of cloud. An unseen owl calls out, reminding every small creature of its beautiful mortality. Shannon takes the last drink, giving a crystal glisten to her lips. I want to kiss her and I think she wants me too, but shyness and the hush of the moon prevails. We head off to our separate rooms, but before turning down the hall, she looks back.

"So, if you want, you could come find me in Denver," she says. "We'll be staying at the hostel there for a while."

Two days later, I'm back on the road heading to the birthplace of Thomas Hornsby Ferril, who wrote, "Corn grew where the corn was spilled / In the wreck where Casey Jones was killed."

Two short rides bring me back to the main road. Walking the shoulder heading south, I watch the daily storm clouds climb over the peaks to darken the sky. My first Vagabond Angel appears, slicing through the rain in a rusted gray pickup. She veers to the side of the road and swings open the passenger door, holding tightly to the collar of an excited German shepherd.

"Where ya headed?"

"Denver."

"I'm going right through. Hop in."

> Vagabond Angel
> appearing as the rain starts:
> Sudden redflower

At that moment, I didn't know that Mary-Jo in that rusted old pickup was a Vagabond Angel, or that there were such creatures. But since those days in Colorado, there have been many road trips and many encounters with these demigods from the pantheon of my personal mythology. They are usually nomadic, but sometimes only psychically so. They are familiar strangers, living poems – loping through fields, highways and smoky bars as if part of the landscape, dancing graffiti leaping off the crumbling bricks of every town I pass.

Since Mary-Jo, there have been many others who have stepped in and out of the scene, who briefly became part of the story, who

Vagabond Song

with a single note changed the melody of my travels, but she was the first I recognized. *My first recorded Vagabond Angel, though I don't remember her real name, the actual color of her truck or even what kind of dog she had.*

We slow to match the pace of an overloaded logging truck in front of us. The rain fades, replaced by the spray off the multiple tires of the logger, keeping the wipers just as busy. Her dog settles between us, his big head resting in my lap.

Mary-Jo lowers the radio and says, "So are you headed to Rainbow, then?"

"To what?" I ask.

"The Rainbow Gathering. I hear it's happening out here somewhere."

"Never heard of it," I say. "What is it?"

"Some big hippie thing. I just figured you were going there. I mean, hitchhiking, long hair …"

"I don't know," I say. "Maybe I am going but just don't know it yet."

"Maybe. So what *are* you doing?"

There's that question again. People are always asking it. What are you doing? Where are you going? What's your destination? Your goal? Your purpose? It's usually asked with a tone of accusation, but not this time. Mary-Jo is different. Her tone is wide open, without a hint of judgment, as if the question means "Tell me about your soul," rather than "Explain your plans for your bank account."

"I guess I'm just traveling. Seeing where the road takes me."

Mary-Jo smiles. She likes that answer.

"Ah, good," she says. "A temporary nomad."

I let her phrase roll around on my tongue.

"A temporary nomad. Yeah, that fits fine."

We bounce down the mountains like a Woody Guthrie ballad and slip into the dirge of Denver-bound traffic on the interstate. All three of us grow quiet and edgy. The soulless red lines of interstates are no place for travelers, no place for Vagabond Angels, road dogs or poets.

These corridors were originally designed, in-part, to move the army and still have a militant, regimented feel to them. They are intended to be used only for transporting rolling steel coffins from one monetized moment to another – having an authentic experience here is highly suspect.

We're soon off the unfreeway and navigating downtown Denver. Mary-Jo drops me at the hostel and disappears into traffic.

I get a bunk in a room with a dozen other temporary nomads. At the desk there's a note from Shannon. She waited a day for me, then moved on. She doesn't say where to, which is just as well – she got me here. Who knows what or who will get me to the next place. What seems to matter is to keep moving.

These city hostels are often more like flophouses than vacation stays. The mood is somber. The beds feel like prison hand-me-downs. The stairwells stink of piss and stale cigarettes. One night here will be plenty.

Five or six nomads sit and stand around a table near my bunk in a lively debate. They're trying to figure out how to get a Japanese deadhead, who speaks no English, to the Rainbow Gathering. So here it is again.

Some are proposing a bus to Glenwood Springs, only $40 then a straight shot down to Bowie, the nearest town to the site of the gathering. But the deadhead doesn't have forty bucks.

"He should go to Boulder," says a guy with a long ponytail and Lennon glasses.

"But that's in the wrong direction," says someone else.

"But it will be easy to catch a ride from there – everyone in Boulder will be headed to Rainbow."

"But Glenwood is more direct."

"But Boulder is a cheaper bus."

"But it's the wrong direction."

They reach an impasse. The deadhead looks from face to face, not knowing what, if anything, has been decided. Suddenly the Boulder proponent spins around and points at me, though I haven't been part of the conversation.

"Do you want to go to Boulder tomorrow?"

I recognize, behind the little round glasses, the eyes of another Vagabond Angel.

"Sure," I say. "Why not?"

"Great. I'll pick you up in the morning," he says, grabbing a jacket and pouch of tobacco. "My name's David," he says, reaching out to shake hands. Then he's out the door.

The table is silent.

Throwing my satchel over a shoulder, I say, "Well, now that that's settled, who wants to grab a beer?"

"I'll go."

"Me too."

"Fuck it. Let's go."

The Glenwood proponent turns to the deadhead and says, "Beer? ... Beeeeer?"

The deadhead grins and gives a thumbs-up. "Beer. Yes, good."

"Yes, good," we all repeat, heading down the hall on our way to a grand night of madness.

> Drinkers in a downtown bar
> delirious with life
> Hailstones drumming
> on the roof of a church

In the morning, David arrives as I'm stashing my mess kit in its proper place in my pack. He rolls a cigarette and sits in the window, smoking calmly – enjoying each deep hit as well as the dance of each curl of smoke blown through the open window. He has about him a palpable lack of impatience. I feel he could sit in that windowsill for days, perfectly content with life.

> Buddha sits smoking
> A Stillness at the center
> of Denver's mad swirl

I finish packing, pleased that everything inside does have its "proper place." This is yet another benefit gleaned from being on the road. The more time I spend living out of a backpack, the more naturally organized the material aspect of my life becomes. It's practical for each item to have its place, as one quickly learns trying to set up camp on a cold, moonless night. Also, it lends a sense of ordered grace to my life, like a Zen garden or the moves of tai chi. It's wonderfully satisfying to be able, unseeing and unquestioning, to reach into a certain pocket and find first aid kit, pocketknife or sewing kit, or into another for compass, sharpening stone or waterproof matches – knowing not just where they are, but also whether the particular item is to the left or right, front or back of its pocket. I have learned to keep my rain poncho not only where I can reach it quickly without having to take off the pack, but where it will protect my maps and hitchhiking signs from a sudden downpour, as well as cushion my neck as I hike. I know to keep my water bottle in the left side pocket so that when I slip off the right shoulder strap, the pack swings the water into my waiting hand and allows a cooling breeze to reach my back, adding to the refreshment.

More than all this, the joy and value of living out of a pack stems from the limitation of available space. I'm forced to carefully consider each item that goes into it. There's no room for the usual trifles that fill and eventually overtake the average American household. People often complain that their space is so cluttered they don't have room to think. Living out of a backpack ensures, at the very least, plenty of room for that.

But it goes deeper than this. Jesus, that hippie-Buddha, Vagabond Angel of Galilee, supposedly said, "Do not lay up for yourselves treasures on earth … but lay up for yourselves treasure in Heaven …. For where your treasure is, there will your heart be also," and "If you would be perfect, go sell what you possess and give to the poor." These words are not so simplistic as to merely suggest that we should be charitable. They are a warning: He knew that possessions will eventually do the possessing, master will become slave and the path will be lost. Shackles and chains have such alluring forms: cars, televisions, electric blankets, credit cards, secure jobs, swimming pools, satellite dishes – each a link binding and burdening until we all become like Marley's ghost: cold souls trapped eternally by luxury and wealth.

"We're chained to the world and we all gotta pull," sings Tom Waits. But not me, at least not yet.

For now, consciously limiting my material goods is an act of spiritual training as important as meditation, study of sacred texts or practicing selfless deeds.

Considering this, it becomes an extremely important decision for me to choose what book to bring on a road trip. For this one, I chose a small paperback collection of the Upanishads, where I read, "Not through much learning is the Atman reached, not through the intellect and sacred teaching," which makes me feel even this book is superfluous.

 David knocks the ember from his cigarette and scatters the remaining tobacco out the window. I slip into my pack and do a quick idiot check around my bunk. Minutes later we're chugging through the outskirts of Denver in David's rusted-out Datsun. I keep my feet away from the hole in the floorboard and my eyes on the rising horizon as we make our way back to the beckoning mountains.

> The road races beneath me
> The sky is still above
> Or it's the other way around
> as the mountains begin to dance

 As we come to a landing in Boulder, I wonder out loud where the hostel is.

 "We can stay at the temple tonight," says David. "Score some good food, too."

 "Temple?" I ask.

 "Hare Krishna," says David. "Did I mention I was a bhakta? A seeker. A devotee of Krishna."

 "You don't look like a Hare Krishna," I say.

 "And you don't look like Hotei," he says, "but you still carry a bag."

 I laugh at the image of myself as the fat, laughing Buddha. When asked the meaning of Zen, he dropped his bag on the ground. When asked the realization of Zen, he picked it up and

Vagabond Song

walked away. Those old-time vagabontaoists were always doing crazy shit like that.

> Drunken lotus flower:
> Jesus wept
> but Kāśyapa smiled
> All the theology I need

The Hare Krishna Temple (technically the International Society for Krishna Consciousness) is a large old house near the edge of town. We park out front and step onto the porch. David knocks softly and we wait. A man opens the door.

"Hare Krishna," he says, greeting us with a slight bow.

He fits the standard idea of what a Krishna looks like. Head shaven save for a ponytail, pale-orange robe, barefoot. He and David exchange a few words in Sanskrit, then the man looks at me with a smile. "Hare Krishna," he says again, bowing deeper. I bow my head awkwardly and repeat the phrase, not knowing what's appropriate. I wonder if he's the head monk here, if he speaks only Sanskrit, if I – a non-practicing outsider – will be welcome.

My doubts dissolve when he breaks from his formal manner and says, "Yeah, man, tonight's going to rock. We've got some killer food and some great drummers are coming for the *Kirtan*. It's going to be cool. Come at six for dinner. You can totally crash here as long as you like."

David stays at the temple to meditate, and I stash my pack and wander off to check out Boulder. All I know of this town is that it's where Allen Ginsberg and Anne Waldman founded the Jack Kerouac School of Disembodied Poetics. "Everything is holy!" declared Ginsberg, and I tend to agree.

Under oak leaves bristling with sun's fire – myriad seismographs of a southwestern breeze – I hover within the music of Boulder. The music comes fully – each note the entire melody, the complete song a single note. Being on the road is perhaps the best practice for living in the Eternal Now. Every moment is new, ephemeral and eternal simultaneously, and nothing is taken for granted. The simple act of walking down Pearl Street becomes a meditation. Each passing person, each stray sound and smell, each movement and flash of color are successive mantras that lead me deeper into the Self, the Unnamed.

> The strewn rose petals
> become a broken taillight
> at the curb, blooming

A drunk argues with himself, a beggar smiles through an iron grate of whiskers, a street clown juggles candy-colored light, a busker bloodies his fingers on blues-laden strings – and in each one I see myself. A spray of rose petals in the gutter becomes broken glass as I approach, and I see it's really all the same: flowers, glass, my flesh, the guitarist's song – separate only in being various movements of the Dance, Lila, reflections of the original face, the one I had before my parents were born.

Back to the temple. After a madly delicious vegan dinner, after the singing, chanting, drumming and readings from the *Bhagavad-Gita*, I roll my bag out on the empty dining room floor alongside David and a few other bhikkhus, most of whom just use a sheet. I can sleep just fine on the forest floor with branches and rocks poking into my back, but the flatness of the hardwood is agonizing. I want to creep out to the backyard and sleep on the good, soft earth, but I'm afraid to wake the others, who all seem

Vagabond Song

to be sleeping without any trouble. Besides, I don't know, maybe in the darkness I would throw my bag on top of some shrine or herb garden. So I stick it out, sleeping fitfully, each position bearable for only a few minutes. When I finally become exhausted enough to fall asleep entirely, everyone is getting up and folding away their sheets.

We climb the hill at the edge of town to chant for the sunrise. Someone lends me prayer beads and shows me how to use them. We chant the Maha Mantra (*Hare Krishna Hare Krishna, Krishna Krishna Hare Hare*) over and over as the sun breaks from the earth and warms our faces (*Hare Rama Hare Rama, Rama Rama Hare Hare*) while we sit, straight-backed and free, if only for an hour. But an hour just may be infinity. Maybe even infinity plus change.

> Temple's hardwood floor:
> yogi that wakes us on time
> for predawn chanting

I find my way to the park, downtown Boulder or thereabouts, and lean on my pack in the long cool grass. Some other travelers are there so we all pool our food and enjoy a good ol' hobo feast: peanut butter and cheese and a loaf of day-old and a stick of salami and canteens of fresh mountain water. Someone has a drum and someone a guitar. Someone has a pipe and someone knows a song.

And just as we came together, we drift off – I to my journal. At a picnic table beneath the same tree I visited the day before, the sweet black ink flows.

> Life lives life
> resonating stories in the drum of my skull
> breathing with the Dance
> for a momentary eternity
> I, breathing dancing living, pause
> for the quickening wind swirling the sky

Under those oak leaves, that canopy of living green veils of the Dance. A sudden cloudburst and the world is washed away, replaced by something new and vibrant. I retreat closer to the protecting tree.

ENTER *another Vagabond Angel.*

(*Like Mary-Jo before him, he appears through a sheet of rain. It drips from the brim of his leather sombrero onto the frayed wool serape that blankets his lean body. Beyond the limits of this cloak are the billowing sleeves of a wine-colored shirt and a pair of knee-high, rain-darkened boots. As we both, in our own fashion, are displaying the traditional garb of the traveler, worn throughout the ages by desert nomads, Romanis, Paleolithic herd-followers, pilgrims, transients, hobos, hippies, yippies, freaks, angels and wayward writers, a connection is felt.*)

ME: You look wet.

PETER: You look dry.

ME: Come on in, but wipe your feet at the door.

PETER: (*laughing, wiping boots on the grass*) Thanks. (*Looking up at the sprawling oak*) Nice place you got here. How's the rent?

ME: Pretty good. My mom's the landlady.

PETER: I think I know her. Big woman?

ME: The biggest.

Vagabond Song

Peter of the Rocks

Fortuneteller in the Latin Quarter
knows nothing about the cards,
knows much about the tourist
& his desire to exchange his money
for an "experience"
granted by this beautiful, mad angel from Ohio

Yes, I know the place, near Dayton,
that gorge just outside of town
some of those boulders
in the middle of the river
big enough to live on

blissful daydream
except for all the schoolkids on tours
yelling and gawking
to see the wildman on the rocks

PETER: So that's how I ended up in Boulder. You?
ME: Pretty much the same.
(*Exeunt.*)

When the rain moves on, so do we. We end up at a Mexican place where, for the price of a Dos Equis draft, we can fill up on free chips and salsa. *La comida de mi pueblo: comida libre.* The conversation turns to this, turns to that, turns itself inside out.

After, walking Pearl Street again. Again, a Vagabond Angel. Parchment-skinned homeless man sits at the top of three redbrick steps, holding court over the street life as jugglers, buskers, dealers and poets dance to the mad music of Boulder. His boots, more worn than Bashō's raincoat, have seen miles beyond midnight, yet I can't imagine him moving from this spot. He is the mythical fixed point around which the universe revolves, resolves itself into a dew and whatnot. Then, miraculously, a kid runs up the steps with a brand new pair of boots. Sits. Gives the boots to the King of the Streets. King slowly removes his old boots, sets them aside. Slowly puts on the new boots, lacing methodically as if the unfolding dream of the universe depends on each movement. Without standing, rocks his feet back and forth to check the fit. Satisfied, he shakes the kid's hand and leans back on his elbows. The kid runs off.

That's the kind of moment one goes on the road to witness. It's the type of vision Williams was talking about when he said, "Now the music volleys through as in a lonely moment I hear it. Now it is all about me. The dance!"

> New boots will someday be
> as worn as the old
> countless miles walked & walked again
> never taking a single step
> & the uni-verse, the One Poem,
> continues to sing itself into existence

A bed at the hostel is $12 a night – a small fortune – and the temple floor doesn't seem like the scene I'm after, so after a couple days it's time to put more miles on my thumb.

Peter wants to go to the Rainbow Gathering. He knows the location: Overland Reservoir, White River National Forest, Turtle Island, Earth.

"What exactly is Rainbow?" I ask.

"It's like Woodstock," he says, "without the electricity or brown acid."

Two women staying at my hostel are on their way to San Francisco to start straight jobs after a summer of actual life. They have a car and a tent. Peter has rough directions. I have a poet's beard and a few words in my pocket. We're off next morning.

Vagabond Song

> A thousand roads lead
> to White River
> but only one road
> will take you there
>
> It's the one you're on
> Always

The road ends at a sea of steel, an immense field glittering with cars and vans. Tents sprout like beachgrass off to the side.

We find a spot to park, grab our gear and make our way to the tents. Empty beer bottles spill from a full barrel. Surly, mean-eyed men prowl like junkyard dogs.

"Is this it?"

"No," says Peter. "This is just A-Camp. The main site is five miles in."

The "A" of A-Camp, it turns out, stands for "Alcohol." They don't allow booze at the actual gathering, but also don't want to turn anyone away. A-Camp is a way for those unwilling or unable to abstain to still participate, and hopefully someday drop the drink and come into the Circle fully. By default, A-Camp dwellers also become parking lot attendants. A fine idea, but unfortunately it results in a gang-like group based entirely on drinking – the energy is violent, tense, ready to erupt. It becomes worse as the days wear on. The way in is no problem, but I'm a little worried about getting back out.

"Dead presidents! Dead presidents!"

We are herded into the back of a rented moving van to be taken the last five miles. As the new arrivals are packed into the windowless box, I'm flashing thoughts of the train to Auschwitz, but follow Peter's lead and climb in.

A shirtless man with wild hair and eyes is waving a coffee can in front of us, asking for donations to cover the cost of the vans.

"Dead presidents! Give me all your dead presidents; you don't need 'em at Rainbow. Everything's free! Everyone's free!"

I stuff a few bills in the can and follow my pack into the cargo hold. A reassuring thought comes to me: if they really were taking us out to the middle of nowhere to kill us all, they'd get our money anyway. Why ask for it now? But then I remember that the Nazis made the Jews pay for their own transportation to the camps. (Dog damn, Nazis are assholes.)

I notice that Peter doesn't put in any money and the guy with the coffee can doesn't pay any notice. Is Peter in on this? All I know about him is what he told me in the park back in Boulder: He came from Yellow Springs to New Orleans, where he made money telling bogus fortunes to tourons in the French Quarter, then to Boulder for the summer writing institute at Naropa. A perfect story of a peace-and-love hobo. Too perfect. That bastard! What is his cut? How much does he collect for each sheep he leads to the slaughter? – Christ, what paranoia! And I'm not even stoned.

"Welcome home, brother!"

My delusions dissolve as I jump off the truck. We're at the foot of a broad valley, green and golden in the late sun. Shoulders of snowcapped mountains border both sides and dotted all around are clusters of tents and tarps, each cluster a separate "kitchen." The hearth is the center of the home here. In the middle of it all is the Main Circle, a gathering and ceremony place where a few hundred people are dancing, meditating, playing music and simply being.

Everyone we pass on the trail greets us with, "Welcome home." At first I think they have me confused with someone they know.

Vagabond Song

Then I think they just don't know I'm a visitor, not a member. Then I think it's some touchy-feely hippie thing I'm too cynical to appreciate. But after a few dozen "welcome homes" my cynicism is outmatched, and I genuinely feel I am coming home. Later in the week, as I hike up to the trailhead to mule in food supplies, I find myself saying it, in complete sincerity, to the brothers and sisters I pass who have just arrived off that same moving van.

The first night, the four of us crash in the tent and I freeze, barely able to sleep. I don't realize until later that this is the beginning of altitude sickness. Chills, insomnia, headache and lethargy are my reward for jumping too high on this crazy 2-ball of a planet.

The next day the women leave, saying this isn't really their scene, but one gives me a phone number to look her up if I make it to the coast. Peter melts off into the swirling masses of Rainbow love, and I go to work on a debris hut. Its insulation will keep me far warmer and more comfortable than the best of tents.

I scan a gentle hillside above Cornucopia Kitchen, looking for the perfect shelter site. One protected from the wind but that still gets plenty of sunlight. One that will drain quickly if it rains. One where the door can face east to catch the first warmth of the morning and more quickly shrug off the night's chill.

I soon find the right area, and then the exact spot: a small lodgepole pine broken three feet up, still partly connected to the stump and angling off to the ground. This will be my ridgepole, so all I need to do is cut off a few branches from below and add them above. I gather more branches and boughs, filling in thin spots. On top of this structure, I add armloads of bark, dry leaves, grasses and sticks – any plant material that will provide insulation. I clear the inside of sticks and rocks, then shove in load after load of soft, dead grass to insulate me from the ground. I make a door plug of grasses clumped between two grates of interwoven sticks then smudge the whole thing with sage, as much to bless it as to keep the insects at bay.

That night I sleep like a king. Better than a king: I don't have to fall asleep in fear that my nightcap of mead has been poisoned.

There is something truly beautiful in an earth shelter, a kind of beauty that all the mansions and palaces of the world will never know. The earth shelter flows with its environment, grows naturally from it and doesn't disrupt its harmony. Most structures of the modern world are cancers upon the earth – their materials are foreign to their surroundings, their shapes are in sharp contrast to the curves and warps of nature, and their concept of comfort is derived from taking one as far away from the natural world as possible. But with an earth shelter, one finds a level of comfort that surpasses all the air conditioners, heated waterbeds and mood lighting of the modern home. It is the comfort of the child in the womb, the egg in the nest.

As I descend further into the chills, fatigue and isolation of altitude sickness, it's the only place I want to be. I'm cradled and warm. I sleep peacefully and wake feeling somewhat better each day.

I slide from my burrow, knocking a shower of pine needles and flakes of bark onto my head. The water in my canteen is icy in memory of the night and the air smells of snow, of elk tracks in crisp white. Winter thoughts in July will take some getting used to.

At the fire, a wire-haired man, curling toward gray, leans back on a log and pulls folk-blues from a guitar as storm-battered as Odysseus' ship and probably with as many miles on it. As the

Vagabond Song

steam from my mug of tea warms my face, he conjures visions of Woody riding the rails of east Texas, singing:

> Go to sleep you weary hobo
> Let tomorrow come and go
> Tonight you're in a nice warm boxcar
> Safe from all the wind and snow

And then the line that gets knowing chuckles from all of us around the fire:

> I know the police cause you trouble
> They cause trouble everywhere
> But when you die and go to Heaven
> You won't find no policemen there

At the end of his song, I rinse out my mug and clip it to my belt. I leave the circle of fire and music to gather firewood. After bringing a few armloads in, I go to work breaking and cutting it into usable sizes, making separate piles for tinder, kindling and fuel. I make this my daily contribution to this family of strangers. The food they give me tastes better and the fire feels warmer when I know that my energy has gone into it. This kind of conscious transfer of energy is what binds me to the flow of life. With the right attentiveness, chopping wood becomes a prayer.

The firewood I deliver to the kitchen is also the only means of communication really open to me. My fatigue and malaise are wrapped around me, blocking every attempt at conversation. I try hiking around the area and swimming in a nearby lake to shake it off, but nothing helps. I accept hits from offered pipes, but that only sends me retreating to my journal and the spider webs of my thoughts. I recall another time, another place, another cold, cold night in a tent.

Wool Blanket

I slept in the valley
shivering, neck sore
from carrying a dead tree
across my shoulders

I needed the wood
but more
I needed the pain

Raccoon wind
shudders brittle leaves
as when you get a sudden chill
and they say:
"someone has just walked
across your grave"

Twig snaps –
& I burrow deeper
wishing I had brought
that wool blanket

glad, almost,
that I didn't

"Shanti Sena! … Shanti Sena!"

The call rouses me. Lifts me from my stupor. I learned earlier this means "peace scene" or "peace doer." The call asks for anyone to come forward as a *Shanti Sena* and help to peacefully resolve a situation. It could be a medical emergency, a fight, a bad trip – any case where someone needs help. The idea is to surround a negative situation with peaceful people and find a solution. In the outside world ("Babylon" the people here call it), cops are called peacemakers, meaning order is restored through force. The cop *makes* you behave a certain way. Here, the focus is on *doing* and *being* peace. It's a creative action, without force or coercion.

"What's wrong?" "What happened?" "What can we do?"

Several people from our kitchen jump up to meet the Shanti Sena, becoming Shanti Sena themselves.

A tall man with blond dreads gathers the crowd around him. "Someone from Babylon came in and attacked a sister," he explains. "He beat her and raped her. She's being cared for, but we need to try to find the guy."

Anger flares through our camp. A couple guys try immediately to rush off into the forest in pursuit, but calmer minds stop them. "We've got to stay in groups of three or more. Stay within hearing range of the others. Search systematically."

"Of course he's from fucking Babylon," an angry voice comes from someone.

"We're all from Babylon, brother. We were just lucky to recognize it and get out."

The people now surrounding the man in dreads lash out in anger. The anger rises to a fury as the crowd grows into a mob. I can imagine hordes of people thrashing through the forest, finding someone they don't recognize and tearing him limb from limb. I can see this beautiful gathering quickly turning into something dark, ugly. All the horrors of the real world, all the anger and fear buried in our hearts erupting, breaking through the façade of peace and unity, spewing venom.

"What do we do when we find this guy?"

"We love him."

I'm floored. The crowd is silenced. The anger blows off like chaff.

We love him. Instantly, an ugly mob becomes a group of caring humans, righteous warriors. Che Guevara wrote: "At the risk of seeming ridiculous, let me say that the true revolutionary is guided by a great feeling of love." In this moment, I begin to understand what he meant.

Without their hatred, what remains in these people is a determination to protect everyone from violence. To find a sick person, not to exact revenge, but to create justice. He won't be harmed, but he will be prevented from causing more harm. Whether that means transforming his soul into light or turning him over to the cops, I have no idea, but I am floored to see peace in action.

We break into groups and fan out into the forest. I scan the tree line and peer into thickets, but I'm hoping I don't find him. Despite believing that the Shanti Sena method makes great sense and is far superior to what America calls "justice," I know I'm not strong enough to love this man. I find myself searching the ground for a suitable weapon. A good stick or rock to bash in his fucking head. I wouldn't, of course. Fear is the constant companion of hate. I stay with my group, but I lag slightly behind, ashamed of my cowardice.

We end up never finding the guy, though everyone is now more vigilant, more protective of this family. The fact that such evil might be faced with the weapon of love is astounding. A hundred Jesuses all around me, but I'm still the Doubting Thomas. This isn't my scene, though I often wish it were. For whatever reasons, my road travels through rockier terrain.

On the 4th of July, everyone gathers at the Main Circle in silence. Thousands of beautiful freaks, freed souls, bhaktas, seekers, lovers, sisters and brothers merging in meditative intention. The energy of the silence builds, swells, becomes a physical force, until high noon, when an "OM" begins, so low and quiet that it isn't heard, only felt. It resonates through us all, becomes audible, grows louder and louder, finally erupting into wild bliss. Drums and bells, dancing singing chanting howling ...

Shake the ground with the night-long dances.
Bacchus afoot and delight abounding!

The celebration flows throughout the day. Costume parades, nude bodies dancing in the sun, music of drums and bells coming from everywhere. I sit on a slope overlooking it all. Humans *being*, with no need for cops or bosses, presidents or priests, city councils or bankers, electricity or oil companies. True anarchy in action. The existence of moments like this must scare the hell out of the Controllers. A lesson in their own uselessness. A testament to the emptiness of each of their justifications for control. As Miscellaneous Jones says, "Revolution: a hundred naked children laughing at God."

In the morning, I pass my shelter on to a young brother who's also without a tent, pack my gear and hike back up to A-Camp. My anticipated trouble among the surly drinkers never materializes – I pass through with only friendly, if slurred, greetings.

Trying to hitch out of the gathering is an absurdist morality play – an endless stream of cars, all of which are willing to pick up hitchhikers, and all of which are already overfull from doing so. I end up walking with a few others, trying for a ride with car after car. We get waves and peace signs and love and songs from each packed vehicle, but no room at any of the motor inns. We walk two miles before finally being invited into the back of a pickup already loaded with four others.

We are a dirty, hairy, stinking pack of singing hobos bouncing along mountain roads and spilling into the streets of Glenwood Springs. I check into the hostel with a couple of others, take a long, hot-as-possible, much-needed shower and emerge a brand new creature. Looking in a mirror for the first time in two months is a bit of a shock. I had imagined that, like Waits, I am merely "in bad need of a shave," but no, this is far beyond that. This is definitely a *beard*. I've never been a man with a beard before and wonder how different the world will be. Something wild stares back at me from the mirror. Something unfamiliar and unknown. Feral. It's not just the beard – the eyes contain a fire I haven't seen before. The skin is deeply tanned from full days of sun. The impression is that of taking a wild animal and bringing it into your home. When someone calls to me to go for food and drinks, I nearly howl in response.

> Among the rocks
> where thermal waters meet the river
> Bodies naked as temple bells
> she swims a kiss to me, flashes away
> I try to hold her mermaid body
> but it dissolves into laughter,
> the water's breath
> & the plea-song of a passing train

Ophelia of the Springs is staying at the hostel with her friend Cissy, and somehow Ophelia and I have fallen into the blissful game of digging each other. We tell our stories while holding hands on the porch. We steal kisses like schoolchildren. When I tell her I'm heading south to stay with friends in Albuquerque, she doesn't want me to go. She has an alternative plan: go with her back home to Colorado Springs, stay with her family for a few days, then hitch south from there. The route is definitely less desirable – it puts me on the interstate, that infected cut into the flesh of the earth where rides are scarce, cops are plentiful and feral beards are anathema. However, the company trumps the route so in the morning we load up Cissy's car and head east.

Going through Vail Pass, we stop at an alpine meadow. In the crisp sunlight she gathers wildflowers for her hair and I gather sage, using thread from my sewing kit to tie it into a smudge stick. I try to kiss her but she pulls away. As we descend the eastern slope the mood in the car cools. The closer we get to the city, the colder she becomes. Before my eyes, the free-love hippie angel transforms into a dutiful daughter of suburban yuppies and the reality of bringing someone like me to her parents' manicured-lawn, three-car garage, glass-coffee-table home begins to sink in. As we near her exit, she pulls the garland of flowers from her hair and says, "I don't think it's going to work having you stay. If we drop you here, you'll be able to get a ride."

Next thing I know, I'm standing by a wall of uptight, rush-hour traffic and she is gone. I left the smudge stick in the car – she'll need it more than I.

After ten minutes of getting angry stares from people coming home from soul-murdering 9 to 5's, I know I'll never get a ride and it's only a matter of time before some cop with a wife-beating mustache is threatening to haul me in. *When you die and go to Heaven, you won't find no policemen there.* I get off the unfreeway and start walking, looking for railroad tracks. The mountains and lakes and rivers now seem like a myth as I walk into Colorado Springs: the Flint, Michigan of the West; the Gary, Indiana of the West; the Midwest of the West. A place full of defense contractors and military bases is bound to have an ugly feel to it. Death profiteers and a gang of thugs that exists to ensure corporate control of the world's resources – definitely the makings of a less-than-friendly populace. I have to get out of here, fast.

I look for train tracks because they will lead me to the poor side of town and that's where the bus station will be.

When I find the tracks, I follow them for a mile or so, watching the surrounding buildings regress from shiny glass horrors to boarded-up brick shells with overgrown lots filling the gaps in their toothy grin – the kind of neighborhood where stray dogs, rats, pigeons and vagabonds are left in peace. Under an overpass, a group of homeless men clusters around a bottle of Mad Dog.

"You guys know how to get to the Greyhound station?"

"Just up that road, three blocks."

"Thanks."

"Got any change?"

I find a small handful in my pocket and drop it into a leathered palm. He looks at me with soul-penetrating eyes.

"God bless you," he says, really meaning it.

"He just did," I say, really meaning it too.

I have a four-hour wait for the next bus, so I stash my pack in a fifty-cent locker and head across the street to a bomb-shelter bar. Inside, I'm the only white person, the only person under fifty, and definitely the only guy with long hair. But I feel right at home. Poverty is a great equalizer.

When I first sit down, I am eyed suspiciously until I order a Coors draft and play Percy Sledge on the jukebox. By the time I leave to catch my bus, I'm down two games to Earl, the resident shark, I'd written a poem in exchange for a drink from Carla the bartender, and I've gotten a half-dozen sloppy bear hugs from Betty, who thinks I look just like her son – only white … and hairy … and skinny … and not in jail.

Vagabond Song

The bus descends through the night
into the bloodstained antiquity of the Southwest
I sleep fitfully, waking in the predawn glow
over red stone & cactus mesas

America is only skin deep –
the flesh of New Mexico is red
One road ends & another begins
as we roll into another myth
that waits for a voice to speak it

caesura: LOON POINT CAMP

THE LAST OF SEVEN SUMMERS AT KEYPAYSHOWINK—a name adapted from the Ojibwa (actually *Anishinaabemowin*) *Kiji-gabeshiwin*, meaning "great campsite." Eleven hundred acres of pines, oaks, maples and cedars surrounding a spring-fed lake flowing into Clear Creek, then to the Tobacco River to the Tittabawassee to the Saginaw to the city where I was born. An artery of water connecting my spiritual homeland to my physical one. Throughout high school and college, I was on camp staff, mostly as the nature director. I once thought I would come back every year, but now I've tasted life on the road. This summer will be my last.

Early Morning, Keypayshowink

> The lake is black glass this morning
> sinewy fingers of fog
> lace along its surface,
> caressing my face and arms

Vagabond Song

> My canoe glides across the silence
> in perfect harmony with its reflection
> & seeing my own wavering image
> pulls me into abstraction
> flesh & bone become fog
> condensed into water
> with the coming of the rising sun
>
> The dew-draped paddle pushes
> from bow to stern &
> after each stroke
> a trail of droplets marks
> the paddle's return:
> goose feathers
> footprints of the fox

In past years I lived in either a tent at staff camp or a cabin down the hill from the dining hall, but this summer I'm living in a tipi, across the lake from everyone else. I'd proposed a new program area that would teach the campers Native American crafts, history and lore. The kids canoe over and make birch-bark baskets, learn the Ojibwa names for animals and trees, light fires with bow drills and listen to stories of Turtle and Rabbit. My teaching area and living quarters are at the tip of a small peninsula where we've set up a woodlands-style longhouse, a sweat lodge and a plains-style tipi – the most comfortable home I've ever known.

On the first morning here I throw open the door flap and startle two fawns browsing on the serviceberry tree in front of my tipi. They scamper several yards up the hill to the protection of their mother, who watches as I push my canoe into the water and jump in. The trio is there almost every morning throughout the summer. I learn to emerge more quietly and they learn to not fear me. By midsummer, I can snack on handfuls of the berries without disturbing their browsing at the same tree.

Wild edibles become the bulk of my diet. Following the deer and raccoons, I browse on blueberry and sheep sorrel, cattail and clover, wintergreen and fiddleheads. I roast acorns and blanch nettles. In the dining hall, I bring a canteen full of lake water and mostly stick to carrots and celery, peanut butter sandwiches and an occasional grilled cheese.

Moving through camp, I use deer trails in favor of human ones. I wear bracken ferns on my head when I discover it keeps the black flies away. I use sweet fern as mosquito repellant, sit chin-deep in the ooze of the swamp to learn from snakes and frogs, carry on conversations with a 300-year-old white pine and a granite boulder dropped by retreating glaciers 20,000 years ago.

The forest is my temple, the lake my altar.

Loon Point (*Gavia Immer*)

> Red stone eye holds the setting sun
> final embers of wildfire &
> all the blood raging in my veins. The loon
>
> erupts beside my canoe fixing me
> forever in that moment with his terrible
> transcendent eye. & his voice:
>
> the laughter of one driven mad
> by the incessant pounding at the door of the world
> *Who's there? in the other devil's name.* His
>
> silhouette in flight mimicked by this
> peninsula cutting halfway across the lake
> giving it a new name known only to me
>
> until now. You too now know the secret
> but you must promise to keep it to yourself
> to use only if you someday come here

STATE RD. 107 & THE MUSIC HIGHWAY
third movement

THIS TRIP WAS TO BE EPIC. The road trip that road trips dream about. A wild ride of luxurious abandon into the heart of hip. Detroit to Memphis. Motown to Beale Street. Fully decked out and equipped in Hunter S. style: a Cadillac Eldorado convertible, a credit card for unlimited gas and food, a sheet of Dr. Owsley's finest and a newfangled video camera to record the madness. My comrades for the journey: Yon Acorn, a former counselor with me at Camp Keypayshowink. Yon reminds me of Hamlet in those rare moments when the prince has cast off his nighted color and his antic disposition is in full-tilt boogie. Also, friends of his: Marta and Juliet, anthousen angels of the suburbs – naiadic nomads in the making. Recently sprung from the Bastille of high school and looking for that first great adventure – the experience that either liberates you to a life on the road (literally or figuratively) or gives you the Big Memory to carry as a hidden talisman through a life of commodified drudgery, aka seeking the American Dream. I was a few years older: the experienced elder

Vagabond Song

traveler, the mentor, the Moses Om to their Zorba Chaos, the Nestor to their Telemachus … the one who could buy beer.

Of course, the road is the real mentor and its first lesson (as always) is the fruitlessness of plans. "Ha-ha-hee-hee!" says Dog. The day before we were to leave, the hammer came down in the form of Marta's mom:

"Get a job on Monday morning or I'm cutting you off."

And just like that, Marta is out, and with her, the portion of supplies that she would have provided. Namely, the Cadillac, the credit card for food and gas, the money for the acid and the newfangled video camera. Suddenly we are three destitute hobos sitting on the floor of my rented room in a former firehouse of downtown Lansing. Gloom and doom and wondering what to do.

"Let's take your car," says Yon.

My car is a '79 Buick with bald tires. It burns oil like a sultan and has more miles on it than East Texas Red. I'd bought it the week before for 200 bucks and a six-pack. A cheap, domestic six-pack at that.

"I doubt that boat would get us to the county line, let alone Memphis," I say, rising and crossing to the window. Incoherent gray and brown shapes crash in from all angles. Hunchbacked buildings whispering lies about their youth. But from the unseen distance, a sound reaches out. That long, lonesome hobo's symphony. *The Sozorogami take possession of me. The Dōsojin beckon me on.*

> & in the train's song
> that shudders past my window
> I feel It again

I smile to myself, the decision made.

"It'll make it," says Juliet. "We'll give it lots of love."

I can't argue with logic like that. "Okay," I say, "but what about gas money?"

Yon has it all figured out: "We go to South Bend and find Geyser." (Another friend from our camp days.) "If we pool our money, we'll have enough for a sheet at a friendly discount and we can sell hits for gas and food along the way."

It's an insane idea. Bat-shit crazy. Bug-nut loopy. Whack-a-doona tuna. It just might work.

"All right," I say, "we'll try to make it as far as South Bend and see how the car is doing. If it's dying, we're not going any farther."

As we load up the next morning, Juliet slips a beaded necklace over the rearview mirror and asks, "So what's his name?"

"Whose name?"

"Your car. You can't take a road trip without naming your car first. It's bad luck."

"I don't know," I say. "I've only had him a week. I don't even know which side the gas tank is on."

"I think it's the bottom side," says Yon, with an antic-Hamlet smile.

Juliet thinks for a moment while patting the dashboard.

"Gus," she says. "He seems like a Gus to me."

"Gus it is, then," I say. "Hello Gus. We sure hope you're up for this trip."

I turn the key and the engine sputters and cranks a few times, then fires. All the gauges look good and from under the hood comes a gentle, perhaps anxious, purring.

"He's ready," calls Yon from the backseat. "Let's hit it!"

Vagabond Song

> Traffic lights shine green
> all the way out of town
> & the radio pulls in Lou Reed
> singing "I don't know just where I'm going,
> but I'm going to try for the Kingdom if I can"
> & we crank it till the speakers complain
> & the road is as clear as the sky
> & we are young & poor & laughing
> & we are happy to be
> three of the Living
> carried like cosmonauts
> across the verses of the universe
> in the arms of a Buick named Gus

We sail across the mono-crops and mohawk-cut woodlots of southwest Michigan and make port in South Bend, Indiana without a flicker of complaint from Gus. Geyser meets us at his door and joins us in the car.

"The whole town is dry, man," he says when Yon asks about hooking us up. "There was a huge bust last week. If anyone has anything, they're not selling."

"What about a bag?" says Yon.

"Nothing." says Geyser. "I'm telling you, it's dry."

"But you have some, right?"

Geyser smiles. "I can roll you a couple of jays. Other than that, I'll have just enough shake for us to smoke a bowl tonight and go see a band."

The band is called Icemakers of the Revolution. A wall of vocal madness reinforced with heavy percussion and a funky bassline. They sing about everything we believe in, are angry about, want to change. We dance our asses off. We sing along to songs we're hearing for the first time. We let our freak flags fly. We are still singing and dancing around the big seats of Gus the next

State Rd. 107 & the Music Highway

morning as we roll out of town, heading south, toward the heart of American music – the birthplace of blues and rock-n-roll.

We stick to the backroads, what Least Heat-Moon calls the "blue highways."

> Fields not yet green
> & trees not yet in leaf
> note our passing
>
> Occasional farmhouses
> hold their secrets
> behind darkened windows
>
> Blankets of blackbirds
> reanimate bone-still trees
> revealing the mystery
>
> But out of context
> & in a language
> we've long forgotten

From the passenger side, the sun glances back at us one last time, then heads off to bed to dream the moon into being. We need a place to crash. Earlier, Yon told us that when we got down south, there'd be caves everywhere for us to sleep in. We're still firmly in the flatlands, though, and the only caves are culverts under driveways crossing irrigation ditches. We drive on in the ebbing light.

"There!" calls Juliet, pointing.

We are coming up on a farm with no lights indoors or out. A few windows are boarded over. The paint on the house, barn and outbuildings is flaked and faded. There are no vehicles and not another house in sight. Perfect. We could stay for weeks, undisturbed, if we wanted.

Hiding Gus as best we can, we slide open the barn door and go inside to find hundreds of straw bales stacked to varying heights. We arrange several bales into a three-person bed with low surrounding walls and cook dinner on Yon's camp stove (insanely dangerous in a barn full of dry straw, but the dogs of disaster, the hounds of horrendous inferno are somehow held at bay). We sit around telling drowsy stories by the light of a candle (even more insanely dangerous, but the puppies of pandemonious blaze are fast asleep, dreaming of wicker rabbits).

We eventually blow it out and settle into our sleeping bags. As the temp dips toward freezing, we snuggle closer to each other and wake in a frosted dawn piled together like a clutch of snakes.

"My feet are freezing!"

"Mine too!"

"We should have kept our shoes inside our sleeping bags. They're frozen."

"Fuckfuckfuck they're cold!"

"Okay," says Juliet, "our feet are cold but our bellies are warm."

"And?"

"We should lie in a circle and put our feet on each other's stomachs."

"That's crazy."

"That's brilliant."

"Okay, let's try."

We take our socks off and form a circle on the bed of straw. I grab Yon's feet, Juliet grabs mine and Yon grabs hers. The thought of ice-cold feet touching my nice warm belly is as terrifying as the thought of a nice warm belly on my ice-cold feet sounds like Heaven.

"One. Two …"

And just for the record, yes, I'm perfectly aware of how ridiculous this all sounds.

"Three!"

"AAAHHHHhhhhhhooooOhmydog that feels good."

A circle of heat and cold that gives and receives, gives and receives, gives and receives until the cold is banished and all that's left is this *warmthgiving* and delirious laughter at the thought of what we must look like. Picturing some farmer walking into his barn to find three freaks practicing some pagan alien mating ritual. Then again, he just might join in. Nobody likes cold feet.

Warmed and shod, we decide to check out the house before leaving. The front door is boarded over, but the back door, hangs ajar on a single hinge. Yon lifts it gently and slides it wide.

Inside it's colder and dust sparkles in shafts wherever light sifts between boards and open windows. Cobwebs drape everything in thick gauze. We wander through rooms that whisper with the ghosts of the people who once lived here. Dust-shrouded furniture mimics gravestones. We can see the dull fog of our breath.

In an upstairs room, in a crate of dirt-caked broken jars, shards of splintered wood and yellowing papers, I find a frayed and spine-cracked journal. The pages, written first in ink, later in pencil, finally ballpoint, record the accounts of a man and his son finding work as itinerant laborers: "Went to work for Geo Mullican Oct. 16 / '60 & worked 35 days at $1.50 for me & 75 cts for my son which amounts to $78.75." Later, he starts his own farm: "1861 Expenses for House Building April 6, paid Legget $15 for stone work. April 15, paid Manyhew $14 for building chimney." The first entry is October 3, 1859. The last entries are undated. The handwriting deteriorates as the years pass.

Vagabond Song

> Yellowed ghost journal
> Autumn leaves crackling footsteps
> Lost bones in the dust

Something about the story held here hits me hard. The idea that a life could be so easily discarded, lost to a bin of rubbish, weighs heavy on me. I feel like I need to try to save the story, reunite it with the living. I stuff the journal into my coat pocket and follow the others back into the sunlight and brittle air of the day. We board Gus and continue south.

"When we get near Nashville," says Yon, "there's caves all over the place. We can sleep in one and check out the city tomorrow."

Night arrives before Nashville does. We hit city limits in the grip of a thunderstorm. The sky is slashed and the pouring rain is biblical. We drive on, never seeing more than the diffused lights of the city, birthplace of Randall Jarrell, who wrote, "Six miles from earth, loosed from its dream of life / I woke to black flak and the nightmare fighters. / When I died they washed me out of the turret with a hose."

With nowhere to stop, no light or clear weather for cave-hunting, no cash for a room, we keep driving through the long night.

In the predawn hours, bleary-eyed and silent, we arrive at Yon's uncle's house somewhere on the outskirts of Memphis. We throw our bags on the floor of a basement room and fall into deep, dreamless sleep.

Waking late morning rounding noon, we drive a golf cart of all things through quiet streets of perfect lawns dotted with pink flamingoes, black jockeys, and more than one Virgin Mary in a bathtub. Across the neighborhood is Yon's grandparents' house, where we are served a Southern breakfast of eggs, grits, potatoes, bacon, ham, sausage, toast, biscuits and gravy and biscuits with chocolate sauce. We stuff ourselves, making up for two days of road food, then drive the cart back to the uncle's and take hard naps till sunset.

Next day we drive into Memphis, home of Johnny Ace, who sang, "May this fire in my soul forever burn," and W. C. Handy, who sang, "Your easy rider's gone where the Southern cross' the Yellow Dog," and B. B. King, who sang, "I want to go home but I ain't got sufficient clothes … doggone my bad luck soul," and Otis Redding, who sang, "It's 2000 miles I've roamed just to make this dock my home," and John Lee Hooker, who sang, "When I first thought to hoboin' I took a freight train to be my friend," and Memphis Slim, who sang, "Feel like a broken spoke in some farmer's wagon wheel," and Jerry Lee Lewis, who sang, "The way is dark. The night is long. I don't care if I never get home. I'm waitin' at the end of the road," and Junior Wells, who sang, "Somebody done hoodooed the hoodoo man," and Alex Chilton, who sang, "Ain't got time to take a fast train. Lonely days are gone, I'm a-goin' home," and Elvis Presley, who sang everything that needed to be sung about love and heartbreak and passion and redemption. And then he started to sing a song only he could really hear. The rest of us were deaf to the cry.

We drive through ghettos of desolation and intense poverty to see Graceland sprawling like a castle of gluttony, reminding the surrounding slums of what they will never have. The message is cruel. All these hearts down here are true. We drive by without stopping.

> Murdered by money
> while the television cameras
> scream out for more
> We keep driving

Vagabond Song

> past the scene of the crime
> with the radio
> turned
> off

Nearly broke for three days in Memphis, we sleep at the uncle's, eat at the grandparents', ride the golf cart past rows of pastel houses and perfectly spaced garbage cans. We might have enough gas money to make it home if we beeline it and eat cheap. No money for Beale Street. "Boss Crump don't 'low no easy riders round here." Being broke in town is to be a vagrant, a ward, a criminal, a ghost. Being broke on the road is to be free.

We know we need to get back out there, but heading home feels like failure. None of us wants to give up yet. We are after something we haven't yet found. Something nameless that's knowable only in the moment of grabbing it.

More road ahead, but the breath is gone, says Kabir. *With desolation in ten directions they move on.*

Long hours in this basement room are taking their toll. Our spirits are sinking and the mood is getting ugly. We'll be taking our frustration out on each other soon. We need a spark and we need it fast.

Yon leaps up from a newspaper with an idea:
"Phish!"
"Fish?" He's lost his mind for sure this time. "You mean catch fish to sell?"
"No. Phish. The band Phish."
"Okay," I say. "That makes even less sense."
"Phish is playing Knoxville tomorrow night. We go hang out in the parking lot where a ton of kids will be selling. We score enough to sell for gas and food."

"Sounds like South Bend all over again," I say.

"No, it'll work," says Yon. "There'll be smoke and doses all over the place."

"Like there were caves all over the place?" I'm being petty but can't turn it off.

"Okay," says Yon calmly, trying to ease through my armor. "How about we leave tomorrow with two goals: find a cave and score some weed. If we fail, we'll go to plan C or D or whatever we're up to now."

"Which is what?" says Juliet.

"Doesn't matter," says Yon. "We're not going to fail."

In the morning, we set sail upon Gus into the rising sun. Back on 40, the Music Highway, connecting the blues to country, giving birth to rock-n-roll. Our spirits rise with the sun – the road is a panacea, tonic to all the ills of the soul. We see a sign for a place called "Bucksnort" and take the exit. Some things just can't be missed.

We drive for a while, never seeing a town, but then we're not looking for one. Juliet points up.

"Look!"

Yon and I look. Breaking from the pines, a rock outcropping shoulders into the sky, and within it, twenty or thirty feet up, is our cave. We park and begin the climb.

> Cave-nestled above something
> called Bucksnort, Tennessee
> on the moonshine run to the state line
> we rest traveling bones, sharing backrubs
> our last joint &
> a rock-framed expanse of impossible colors
> lapis sky,
> tsavorite forest,

Vagabond Song

> sapphiric stream carrying
> all of this, & us, into the Now
>
> Beyond our view stretches Highway 40
> removed from Earth
> by much more than paralytic legs of concrete –
> steel boxes race along it
> cutting the fabric of our silence
> but feebly, like the bill of a tern
> on the sail of a brigantine,
> easily ignored, easily forgotten
> until necessity puts us back
> into our own box of steel
> & we cut our way toward Knoxville

We roll into town realizing we have no idea where the concert is being held, so we head downtown looking for the Scene.

"There's some kids," calls Juliet, pointing out some long-haired, thrift-store-bedecked guys shuffling down the sidewalk. "Kid" being the latest term for the current generation of hippie/freak/beat/bohemian/beautiful-free-child-of-the-earth. A "sweet kid" is the modern incarnation of a "righteous hippie."

We pull over, jump out and follow. We know the kids will lead us to the local coffeehouse – not a café, but a good old coffeehouse with wild art on the walls, an overloaded bulletin board promoting house shows, poetry readings, lost bikes, political rallies, puppet theater and roommates wanted. The music will be loud, refills will be free and it will be full of sweet kids who will all know how to get to the Phish show.

The first guy we talk to gives us directions, half his bagel and his number in case we need a crash pad. The kids are *still* all right.

At the show, we work the lot scene like floor traders on Wall Street but it *is* South Bend all over again. No doses. No shrooms.

No smoke. Nada. Except for a kid sharing balloons of nitrous, there seems to be nothing to be bought, bartered or begged. South Bended. *Oh Lord, stuck in South Bend again.*

One guy we ask says he doesn't have drugs but he has tickets. The next few say the same thing. Someone had printed passable fakes. Five bucks a pop, but when we explain our financial straits, we get three for ten, give up on scoring and go in to enjoy the show.

The music is a trip of its own. Jam with an ear for jazz, danceable lunacy, fractillian chameleonosity. There's something beautiful about catching a band at the perfect point on their arc: they love what they're doing, they and their fans are one – both feeling and being the music, no one's jaded, burned out or fame-infected yet. The media hasn't noticed anything to hype and exploit yet. Performer and listener are in the same tribe, dancing around the same fire. It's easy to diss on Phish and jam bands in general, but this is totally beside the point. It doesn't matter if one thinks their songs are "good" or "bad" or any other relative judgment. What matters is this moment they create. This ride they provide.

We're still high on it all when we get to the crash pad. Rather than coming down, we join the circle around a tapestry-draped coffee table to enjoy a red glass bong that goes round and round and round and then – What is *this* music?

The crackle of needle on vinyl gives way to a distant piano, drums, then the call to prayer of the unmistakable trumpet of Miles Davis. But this is no *Kind of Blue*. Is this even jazz? Is it even human? Someone hands me the album cover. The artwork dances with the heavy basslines and the bopping electric piano. Flaming lotus hair becoming sky becoming sea exultant naked African glory gazing to horizon and beyond. Lightning-strike

Vagabond Song

surf-crash and then that trumpet again. Rising, climbing the sun highway, tumbling over clouds, Icarus with wings impervious to heat, creating their own heat, heat that dances with the sun's. I stare at the woman, sweat-dappled face in profile, and urge her to look my way. Beg her. She refuses. An ocean of percussion, drums and that piano crash on every shore of my brain and body, giving way to a heartbeat bass and I'm back at the beginning – the horn – is it a call to prayer or war? Is there a difference? The only true war is the one fought inside your skull. *Penuel.* The bass and guitar take me in a fast ship across choppy seas wind snakes my hair Medusa smiles duck into cave underground sea calm without wave or light the ship floats free into the black gently guided by the rippling horn disembark on sunless beach ghost crabs scurry underfoot with heartbeat bass again then dancing to fires writhing on the black sand creatures retreat eyeless to clefts in the rock fires dim almost extinguish the bass and piano discuss death until that damnedblessed horn blasts the beachfires into the sky to become stars. We all become stars. All become stars. All become … silence.

> Waking on a living room floor in Knoxville
> sun tapping at the windows
> ears still echo with *Bitches Brew*
>
> Miles Davis has changed my life, again
>
> We'll head north today
> having reached the furthest possible point
> on a journey into casual madness
>
> One can only push these things so far
> before "going home" becomes a myth –
> a fairytale for winter campfires
>
> Stars telling stars of stars

Two days later I'm back in Lansing, trying to write a book that will take another ten years and many more road trips to understand and even then I'll get it all wrong. Juliet stays with me for a couple of weeks, having apparently run away from a less-than-satisfactory reality back in that Stepfordian suburb north of Detroit. She's trying to track down her brother, who is somewhere on the road. After a dozen phone calls, tips and blind guesses, she finds him in California and decides to hitch her way out to meet up with him.

I don't like the idea of her hitching alone. I hate that we live in such a broken society that it's dangerous for a woman to be on her own – everyone has the right to solitude and solo flights into adventure. It isn't so much that the roads are filled with predators, but that the media hypes a twisted fabrication to sell papers, movie tickets and all the useless crap of TV commercials. Mostly they're selling fear. Fear is the greatest tool of control. Control is the greatest tool of profit. For the thousands of stories of kindness and generosity of hitchhiking, there may be one of violence, but every story told by a movie, newspaper or network broadcast is negative. It's part of the very successful American brainwashing system that results in nearly everyone you talk to saying, "Hitchhiking? Oh, that's really dangerous." Yet no one ever has any evidence of this danger.

In the late '30s, a rash of anti-hitchhiking laws was sponsored by transportation companies, who wanted to stop the free rides and sell tickets instead. The AAA started a campaign called "Thumbs Down on Thumbers" and, with the help of that Gestapoist criminal J. Edgar Hoover, flooded newspapers with stories of psychopaths, rapists, murderers and sex fiends prowling the highways. Of course, these stories never named names – they

Vagabond Song

were filled with anonymous anecdotes, i.e., lies.

There's another goal at work here beyond profit motive. It's about control of information. When the news is controlled by pro-corporate, anti-worker interests, an alternative communication system is needed. Historically, it was hitchhiking. A witness to a strike or strike-breaking activities could spread the word coast to coast with a thumb – the first internet. The stories that the official press wouldn't cover, or plain lied about, were being told person to person. An anti-hitchhiking smear campaign suited the bosses and their political lapdogs perfectly.

Sixty years of this has convinced the average person of the dangers of hitchhiking, but a byproduct of this pornographic hyping of a lie is that many men who see a woman hitching think the movies they've watched and stories they've read are true and obviously, if she's asking for a ride she's looking for sex, too. That's how all the stories go. It's when the lie hits the wall of truth that something ugly can happen. A man who otherwise would behave acts out on a false fantasy, and the woman finds herself, yet again, having to deal with the bullshit. She finds herself in danger. The lie of the corporate/governmental/entertainment complex becomes a self-fulfilling prophecy.

So I am reluctant to see Juliet go off alone even though I feel this may be as sexist and controlling as the imagined man I'm protecting her from. She promises to call as soon as she meets up with her brother. She wears a good knife on her belt. She's young but absolutely not naïve. So in the end, I drive her out to an entrance ramp and hug her good-bye.

I wait in Gus until a car pulls over to pick her up. The guy seems friendly. No gut alarms are going off. She chats with him at the window, waves back to me and hops in. There's nothing I can do now. She's free, and freedom is always risky. I have to believe the Dōsojin will take care of her.

They do.

She calls a week later, reunited with a brother she hasn't seen in years and enjoying the California sun. She also calls her parents, who apparently were fine with her leaving – one less damn kid to worry about.

A year later, the Minneapolis police steal Gus off a side street and throw him in the impound lot. I had given him to Francisco when I left for Mexico, but the plates expire while I'm gone. They want $300 to get him back. When I return to the States, Francisco and I drive out to the impound lot to get our belongings out of him, including Juliet's beaded necklace from the rearview mirror. In the thick dust of the hood I write his epitaph, the same as Rudy's from *Ironweed*: "Gus. He knew where the Milky Way was."

interlude

It's rumored they met once,
Zorba Chaos & Miscellaneous Jones,
out beyond the tracks
where the Cunningham boy was found
Jones chewing on a hickory switch
& Zorba smoking hundred-dollar bills
in a corncob pipe
Jones had a map of the Hi-Line
painted on a buffalo hide
Chaos had a tattoo of a white whale
on the side of his neck
Nobody knows what they talked about
but one thing is certain:
Both were smiling as they topped the hill,
passed the old Gibbons Place
& went their separate ways

M-46
fourth movement

THE THIRD SEMI IN A ROW THUNDERS BY blasting me with road grit and shuddering through my worn coat. I'm on the wrong road. I should have taken 18 to 61 to 13 – two-lane strolls through quiet towns with names like Prudenville, Gladwin and Kawkawlin, where old men with six-packs of Schlitz or Black Label pick you up and tell stories of hitching home after the war. Instead I'm on U.S. 27, a divided, limited-access unfreeway where cars go too fast to see your eyes and you're supposed to stay at the top of the ramps, behind the "Motor Vehicles Only" sign, which limits your chances to only that rare car entering at that one ramp.

"Motor Vehicles Only" – painful as a gut shot. So, of course, you have to ignore that and walk down to the road proper and hope against hope that someone will pick you up before the Highway Patrol does.

As I spit the dust from the passing truck, it occurs to me that yet another piece of the romance of the American road has been destroyed by the life-sucking interference of the insurance com-

Vagabond Song

panies. The trailers the truckers pull are often owned by a corporate octopus with lawyer and insurance agent barnacles gripping every tentacle. Hitchhikers are a risk, an excuse not to cover a claim, so for the drivers they are a threat of job loss. Thus the stories of hobos and truckers sharing stories become just stories. A thing of the past, like ten-cent coffee and original thoughts. Big Joe is under surveillance and the Phantom 309 is the property of the suits and briefcases.

"Capitalism kills romance!" I yell into the dust-echo of the truck. "Truckers never pick up hitchhikers, it's all a damn lie!"

As if on cue, a semi pulls to the side of the road, exhales grandly and waits. For a moment, I ponder the possibilities: This is a mirage, telling me I've been too long on the road, too long in my own thoughts. Or, I have manifested the truck merely by the power of thought, a stunning example of quantum psychosis and psychokinesis. Or perhaps St. Christopher is also the patron saint of irony. Whatever the explanation, I shoulder my pack and run for the cab.

> One thousand trucks pass
> as a steel claw cloud
> scrapes sparks across the sky
>
> One thousand trucks
> But the one that stops:
> Sunlight dancing willow

"Welcome aboard!"

I climb up and stow my pack between my feet. The driver is thinner than most truckers I've seen bellied up to steak and eggs at countless truck stops across the country. A seed company hat is nestled between two sprouts of wild, wheat-brown hair. Winter wheat. His nose looks like it has seen the wrong end of a fist more than a few times, but his eyes dance with no sign of regret from beneath wooly brows.

"Name's Clyde. Pleased to meet ya. Where ya headed?"

"Saginaw."

"Me too." Clyde nods. "Where 'bouts?"

"Old Town," I say. "There's a payphone there I use to let friends know I'm back in town that just happens to have my favorite bar wrapped around it."

I notice right away that Clyde is generous with his laughter and this has him going for a full minute. It's infectious. As our laughter subsides, he explains that he has to drop his load at the stone docks just outside of town, but if I didn't mind the wait, he'd drop me at my bar afterwards.

A free ride comes with an obligation. It's your job to either talk or listen. To entertain with a story or to receive one. Clyde has stories that need a good ear.

"Been drivin' truck 'bout six years now. Guess it's all right, but it's not what I really want. See, I'm a farmer, always was. Whole family always was far back as anyone knows. I love workin' the land. Christ, biggest rig I ever wanted to drive was a John Deere tractor. But it got so's I couldn't make a livin'. Everything goes up and food prices go down. What kinda trouble we in when ya can't afford to farm?

"So I started drivin' just part time to pay the bills. Pretty soon I'm drivin' all the time and no time for farmin'. Tried to put in a few acres a' corn at least for a while. Then I just kept a little veggie patch up by the house. This year, I didn't even do that."

We're both quiet for a while, passing fresh crops of subdivisions infesting what was once farmland. Uniform rows of lifeless boxes, pale and overgrown, cancerous. A maze of winding streets between the chem-green lawns, named for trees or birds that are no longer there.

Clyde laughs a staccato note to break the silence. "Christ, drivin' truck's okay, though. Could be worse, I could be livin' in one of them fancy prison camps over there."

We pull off the highway and chug down a gravel road heading toward the river. At the gate, we're directed to a large building with immense, open bay doors that we drive through and stop alongside a front-end loader. Towering piles of limestone, ranging from boulder to sand, create an alien landscape. An office projects from the north wall into the loading area.

"Should be 'bout a half hour," says Clyde, opening his door and dropping out. "If you need to hit the head, it's through them doors."

I climb from the cab and go outside to have a look at the river. Across a barren, hard-packed expanse where great hills of gravel and stone rise in defiance of the surrounding flatlands, the Saginaw River drags its brown body through industrial decay, heading toward the redemption of the Bay and Lake Huron beyond. "Saginaw," contrary to a popular legend about the Sauk, who never lived here, derives from an Anishinaabe word meaning "place where the waters flow out." Emerging from a vast wetland known locally as "the Flats," several rivers and streams join forces to become the two main rivers, the Tittabawassee and the Shiawassee, that then merge to form the Saginaw. They once provided an abundance of food for the people who lived here: fish and waterfowl, scores of wild edibles and the richest of soils for game-filled forests and immense gardens.

Today, the rivers are clogged arteries killing this land. The

Shiawassee brings runoff from crops poisoned by Monsanto and Cargill, the Flint River adds toxins from General Motors and the Cass River brings more pesticides, herbicides and chemical fertilizers. The Tittabawassee has been attacked by dioxins from Dow Chemical and, via the Pine River, by a host of pollutants from the Michigan Chemical Corp. (Now Velsicol, the "technology leader in industrial intermediates based primarily on cyclopentadiene including hexachlorocyclopentadiene and chlorendic anhydride." Now *there's* a slogan to rally around.) Once a paradise teeming with fish, the Saginaw River now has signs posted at every dock and pier warning people and stating advisable limits of consumption: "DO NOT EAT Carp and Catfish / Women and Children: White Bass – six meals per year, Walleye – one meal a month if under 22 inches …"

I grew up along these banks and have this death-water in my blood. We all do.

>River's brown scar
>cuts between past & present
>We attempt the crossing –
>spend day after day
>searching for our own grave
>
>A solitary gull
>comes to rest on its own reflection
>dapples at the frail skin of time
>while we die of thirst
>with a mouthful of water

Clyde calls to me, pulling me back to the world. We load up and head into the streets of Saginaw, birthplace of Al Hellus, who wrote, "I'm naked in soul, bone deep in questions."

At Ewald's I make my call: "Hey, man, I just got in.… Yeah,

Vagabond Song

Ewald's. Ma's working tonight.... It was smooth sailing.... There was this great trucker.... Yeah, I know, a trucker.... Let's shoot a game and I'll tell you about it."

 While waiting for the friend to arrive, I grab my favorite table, with its bridge-view window, and sip on a free draft (thanks, Ma!), broke and trying to make it last. The place is nearly empty, just how I like it. No distractions while descending into the waters of my journal, into the undertow of the poem. I watch the sad dance of futile flirtation by the poor bastard at the bar.

... What You Want

> We've all been Jeff Goldblum's character
> in *The Big Chill*,
> which gives us sympathy
> for the awkward guy at the bar
> failing to impress the bartender
> w/ stories of his youth & off-key
> snatches of song w/ the jukebox
>
> & we've all been Glenn Close, too
> which is why we find ourselves
> from time to time
> crying in the shower
> where no one will hear &
> the salt of our tears will never reach us
>
> & one day, we will all be
> Kevin Costner's character
> dressed by strangers & receiving
> only half a eulogy
> but then again, as the organ hums,
> "you can't always get ..."

M-46

A couple nights of catching up with the old Jefferson Avenue gang, late-night jam sessions with guitars, hand drums, a flute and me banging on pots and pans, stovepipes, glass ashtrays – anything I can get my hands on – while throwing out scraps of unwritten poems. They catch fire in the air and nothing but ash remains.

A couple mornings at the Red Eye with the greatest baristas, the most surreal conversations and the best coffee in the world, or cheap eggs, hashbrowns and toast at Pete's Grill, the last of its kind in a world that's the last of its kind. But then the call of the road grows too strong to ignore and I head west on one of my favorite runs: M-46, two lanes of possibility that slice sideways across Michigan's wool mitten like a dropped stitch. It's autumn, the season when nostalgia and romance dance a two-step through every smoky bar of the imagination.

A first short ride gets me out of town and leaves me standing in front of an abandoned schoolhouse turned antique shop turned boarded-up silence. A wind tasting of snow sweeps across gray fields of ghost corn and the detritus of the sugar beet harvest. A car passes. Then another.

The sky has been darkening since an uncertain morning, and now, with a sudden leap in the wind, the rain begins – a few stinging drops soon building to a barrage. I pull out my poncho and throw it over myself and my pack, looking like a hobo Quasimodo. The wind-torn rain slashes relentlessly at the only figure it can find on this road.

Only the Dead

"Only the dead have seen the end of war." –Santayana

Part One: The Voice

The sky too is concrete
rain whipping cold like a father's belt
& I stand, thumb in hand,
waiting
for that one good ride

This is where it begins
This is where it will end:

A boy sways in the grip of a dying tree
turns away for a moment
& finds himself, a grown man planted
in the gravel of another road –
a crow perches on his heart
an owl on his tongue

This is where it begins
This is what I've become:

Western highway fading south
boots lapping up the puddles
like thirsty dogs
eyes squinting into the torrent
of black black rain

I am grateful for the weight of my pack
& the icy thunder all around

& then the welcome smile of brake lights
& I'm trading stories w/ a farmer turned trucker
& opening my coat against the heat
& the miles peel away like dollar bills
& the stillness returns
& with it, the haunting words

chanced upon in a photograph
in our illegal attic:

"Only the dead
have seen the end of war."

Sometimes it all comes together
to form what we call a moment
& the moments line up
like schoolchildren
to become a memory –
cluster of images,
fury of autumn leaves

& in this moment, now,
it suddenly occurs to me:
I have never in my life
left a forwarding address

Years later, years before, seeing that photo Francisco had tacked up to the wall of Symposia, our invisible wrinkle on the map of reality – and later that night, jazz at the Loring and that bass player pounding it into my gut with each big note: Only. The. Dead. … Only. The dead. Gone our hope for peace, gone our lion and lamb. Only the dead. … But then again, which war, which death? The struggle with oneself, Jacob wrestling the angel, the great internal, eternal battle to remain free and true – when this war is forgotten in order to grab a paltry peace, we are no longer truly living, we are merely the pleasantly moaning, walking dead who comprise the vast horde of humanity. Life is struggle. Sisyphus rolling that beautiful stone up that gift-giving hill. Fight on, comrades! Hoka hey! Sleep with your boots on! Show no quarter in the war against the mundane, and as the stone rolls back down the hill, take a moment to enjoy the view.

Vagabond Song

       Part Two: The Cry

    America, land of the big backyard
    & swimming pools
    self-induced lobotomies
    thirty-one flavors
    & neon, dayglo electric chairs
    if only I weren't born within the golden bars
    of your Fourth Reich,
    if only I weren't born in the shadow
    of your Roman eagle
    I could love my country
    the way Neruda loved Chile
    or Kazantzakis loved Greece
    but you've made it impossible
    to separate land from state
    people from policy
    geography from government
    & so to be an American poet
    is always to be a poet without a country
    because a poet is nothing
    if not a teller of truth

    & we gather in fields of broken glass
    We love the weeds that splinter the sidewalk
    We, following Whitman,
    sound our barbaric yawp & wear our hats as we please,
    indoors
    or out
    & everywhere
    we gather on rooftops
    drinking rainwater
    from rusty eaves

    Only the dead have seen the end of war
    but not all wars are fought
    w/ the guns & bombs
    of the weak desperation of empire –
    the flag-waving children of Babylon

> Sometimes the moon
> is the only witness to murder
> & she would never
> rat out her friends

I climb into the cab and slam the door against the onslaught of rain.

"Thanks for the ride—"

"Are you Marc?"

For a moment it flashes through my brain that my name is becoming known on these roads, a subject of half-believed tales told at rest areas and truck stops, a semi-mythological creature that brings good luck to weary travelers or at least a good story to keep them awake as they go from Point A to Pointless elsewhere and beyond. But no, it's not that. ... my anonymity is still intact, thank Dog.

"Clyde?"

"Welcome aboard, again."

Again that same easy laughter, that open smile. The first and only time a Vagabond Angel has struck twice.

Part Three: The Wilderness

> This is where it will end.
> This is where it begins:
>
> Flowers
> unbloom
> themselves
> in muddy progression

> the wind picks up
> & all I want
> is another
> cup
> of coffee

The storm is on its own road, and after another hour it catches a ride heading east. The sun breaks free from the gray prison of cloud.

Clyde points out passing crops, ones he used to grow.

He says, "I loved farmin'. Work was hard but real. You work with your hands, you work with the earth, and you know your life means somethin'. You can feel the meanin', the truth of it, in your sore muscles. Life gets under your fingernails 'long with all that dirt. But like I said, I couldn't make it pay. Drivin' truck pays good, but there's no time for farmin'. I put nothin' in this year. Not even a little kitchen garden. Not even a single tomato."

He sinks into silence. One of the most important skills of hitching is knowing when it's time to just look out the window and listen to the sound of the engine as the miles peel away.

A vee of migrating geese gets Clyde talking again.

"Look at them go. No bags, no passports, headin' south for the winter. They're the smart ones. That's what I shoulda done – git while the gittin's good, as they say."

"You ever do any traveling?" I ask.

"Nope," he answers. "Sixty-three years and I've never been farther than Chicago. What about you? Even been out of the country?"

"Just Mexican border towns, but that doesn't really count."

Clyde looks over at me, studying for something, then speaks. "You're young yet. You should go while you still can."

"Where?"

"Anywhere."

It occurs to me then that he is right. I remember a friend from my college days who told me her sister ran a school in southern Mexico, near the Guatemalan border. She said if I ever wanted, she could hook me up with a teaching gig there. Soon as I can, I'll look her up and get an address.

Clyde begins braking and downshifting, "Here's my turn. I'll drop you by that big tree in case it rains again."

"Thanks," I say. "Next time you pick me up, I'll tell you all about my trip to Central America and who knows where else."

"Deal," smiles Clyde. "I sure would like to hear about that."

M-46, October

> Clyde's old diesel
> rolls to a stop
> and I hop from the cab
> onto a protest of gravel
> beneath my duct-taped boots
>
> an autumn flourish of blackbirds
> slashes across the road before me
> a scurry of suicide leaves
> mirrors from the other side
>
> a gateway leading
> to the next ride
> the next story
> the next splash of paint
> on the canvas of my travels

interlude

And here's something else:
When Robert Johnson went to the crossroads,
two people met him there –
the Devil, in a fresh-pressed silk suit,
dahlia in his lapel, sitting behind the wheel
of a cherry-red Cadillac,
& Miscellaneous Jones
with a walking stick & a straw hat

We all know what the Devil promised,
but whatever deal he made with Jones,
Mr. Johnson took that secret
to his lonely, barking grave

The Chicken Bus Highway, Part I
fifth movement

I WAKE TO THE SOUND OF GUNFIRE. Staccato trills of machine guns and the hollowed thud of mortar shells. The Zapatistas have arrived.

They first made their existence known in the mountains around San Cristóbel, four hours to the north. They swept through villages like the spring rains – sudden, overwhelming, cataclysmic. The newspapers, on tight strings of the Mexican government, told us they were Guatemalan communists led by a German anarchist – catching all the favored boogeymen and ethnic triggers in one fell swoop.

The rumor creeps in: they'll come here next because we have an airport. The international students have all been evacuated to Mexico City. The first piece of graffiti I've seen here appears one morning. A friend translates it as "Tapachula, you're next." *Los Tigres*, the too-young soldiers on downtown street corners gripping automatic rifles and with shaky hands, are more on edge with each passing day.

I ask Doña Anna if we should be worried.

"Oh, it's nothing," she says, popping a mango slice into her mouth. "We have a war every few years, but we just keep on with things."

I find this less than reassuring.

Doña Anna and her husband Humberto run the school where I've been living and teaching. She's from the States, a former beat poet, photographer and fashion model. He's a former bullfighter. They met in Mexico City in the late '50s, fell in love and traveled the country to find the right place to start a school. The found Tapachula, nearly at the southernmost point of Mexico, land of the Mam people of the Maya.

My journey here, less romantic and more recent, has been a comedy of terrors.

After Clyde's advice to travel outside of the U.S., I tracked down a friend from my college days, Anna's sister, who I knew through weekly Bahá'i Firesides held at her home. I was still, in those days, clinging to the idea that a valid spirituality could be salvaged from the wasteland of organized religion and the Bahá'i precepts of equality of the races and sexes appealed to me. The Firesides were informal discussions that felt more philosophic seminar than religious gathering and the snacks and tea offered was often my only meal of the day. But when talk of joining the faith began to slip in among the Descartes and chamomile, I knew it was time to move on.

Two weeks after reconnecting, I fly from Detroit, home of Faruq Z. Bey, who wrote, "I'm a nomad in this land called Fear," to Mexico City, home of Octavio Paz, who wrote, *"Tal vez busca su destino. Tal vez su destino es buscar."* – "Perhaps he searches for his destiny. Perhaps his destiny is to search." It's the day after

The Chicken Bus Highway, Part I

Christmas. I have about $200 to my name and know only two things in Spanish: how to swear and how to order a beer. Before the day is done, I use the first profusely and don't have enough money left for the second.

Traveling with my old friend, the army-surplus canvas backpack, as well as my dad's matching duffle bag that he took to Okinawa and a suitcase holding a typewriter named Moonstar, I arrive, pass through customs and change my money. I load my gear and hobble out to a line of cabs.

"Ess-stass-ee-own day auto-boos, poor favor," I say, stumbling through the pages of my guidebook.

"Which one?" smiles the driver in passable English – miles beyond my Spanish. "*Hay quatro. There's four.*"

Chinga. Now what? I thought I was heading south, but it's actually more to the east. Two different bus lines go to Chiapas and we almost settle on the wrong one. Finally the driver figures out I'm going to Tapachula and tells me the station is called "*TAPO.*" He then swindles me out of a good chunk of my cash. I know he's doing it, but I'm confused by the mix of new pesos and old pesos. Earlier in the year, to deal with the heavy devaluation of the currency, they knocked off three zeros, so 1000 old equals one new but both bills are still in circulation. I hand over too big a wad of old and new, swindled but not fluent enough to make my case. I shrug and smile like the dumb gringo I am.

By the time we reach *Estación TAPO*, I have confused the word into *tope*, which, because San Cristóbel is a comedian, means "speed bump." "Take me to speed bump, *por favor.*"

I mule all my luggage into Speed Bump and get in line. After an hour of the slow crawl to the front, I put my money on the counter and say, "Tapachula."

"*Mañana.*"

"No, no, no. I want to go today."

"*¿?*"

"Um ..." I fumble through the guidebook. "*Hoy. Necesito hoy.* Today."

"*Hoy no hay. Mañana.* Bus already go today. You go tomorrow. Tapachula."

Chinga. Chinga. Chinga. Now what?

I buy a ticket for mañana and stash most of my gear in a locker. Outside, I approach another cash-eating cab. I need a cheap hotel, nearby. I blunder my way through the guidebook again.

"Ness-ay-seeto une otel, muy despass-ee-o, sirka day a-key."

He points to his map, a spot several zones away. Is he trying to get me for a longer ride and a bigger fare or is it that the hotels around Speed Bump are too pricey? I mumble and stumble and *habla* and parley but still he points to the same place. Fine.

"Bweyn-o. Ba-mouse."

We blast into the tumult of traffic. Four-lane streets with cars six and seven abreast, everyone speeding weaving honking dodging, running red lights, jumping from clutch to gas to brake to gas like a berserker dance party, and I'm sliding around the backseat trying to learn how to pray in Spanish. My driver maneuvers like a matador and drops me, wobbling and lost, at the doors of a hotel I can't afford.

I suspect as much as soon as I enter the gilded lobby. The red velvet drapes eye me disdainfully. The epaulet on the shoulder of the bellhop peers down its nose at me. The desk clerk tells me the price. Forty pesos more than I have. Anywhere. In the world. ... *Chingaaa.*

I ask for a cheaper hotel and he sends me two blocks down to

The Chicken Bus Highway, Part I

a place that doesn't look any more promising. I have enough, but barely. As I pay, I realize that I won't have enough left for a cab ride back to Speed Bump in the morning. That should be interesting. Well, mañana. *Que sera* and all that.

My room is on the larger size of shoebox, maybe 11s or 12s. A single window looks onto a vista of brick walls and garbage bins. I go out for a walk, touring crumbled buildings and gaping potholes from the '85 earthquake. Twenty minutes later my eyes and throat are burning from the smog. I retreat to my room, dine on trail mix and go to bed.

> Sirens & smog scratch
> at the window through the night:
> Screeching alley cats

In the morning, I ask which local bus will take me to Speed Bump. For some reason the desk clerk is confused by my question. Eventually he seems to figure it out and tells me the bus number and where the stop is. I walk down to the bus stop and watch four buses blast by several lanes from the curb. They all have the same number as the sign I'm standing next to, but they don't stop. By watching the locals, I finally figure out the method: When my bus is approaching, I dart toward it through the racing traffic. The driver sees me and slows down, opening his door. I jump in, and he slams the door and guns it. And, of course, it isn't the right bus.

"¿A donde vas?" says a voice from the back of the bus after I try to ask the driver if he goes to Speed Bump.

"Ess-stass-ee-own day auto—"

"English," he says.

Oh, thank Dog. "The bus station for Tapachula. I think it's

called *Tope.*"

"No, no, no. It's *TAPO*. It stands for T*erminal de Autobuses de Pasajeros de Oriente*. *Tope* is a speed bump."

"Well, that explains a lot of very strange reactions."

The man laughs, then makes the driver stop and refund my money. He gets off with me, walks me to a corner and says, "A bus will come this way soon. It will take you straight to your station."

Hay ángeles en todas partes. There are angels everywhere.

I get to the station, retrieve my gear from the locker, get on the Tapachula bus and begin the descent into suffering. Twenty-one hours of cramped seating, sweltering heat, sweating bodies, bad roads – still dressed in clothes for a Michigan winter, having had nothing to eat but a tub of trail mix for two and a half days, wondering just what the hell I've gotten myself into this time. Somehow, finally, we arrive. I drop my last few centavos into a phone and call Anna at the school.

She suggests grabbing a cab, and I tell her I don't have money for one. I assume she'll come get me, but instead she says she doesn't have money for a cab either. Her husband is off on one of his mystery trips again, sometimes lasting a couple days, sometimes weeks. He apparently has a habit of getting up before dawn and disappearing without a word. It doesn't seem to bother Anna at all. However, since she isn't a citizen, the bank account is in his name and she can't get any money until he comes back. Whenever that might be.

"But you can walk. It's only ten blocks."

So I packmule myself again, and set out in the ninety-plus heat, far overdressed for the climate, trudging down long streets with nearly two-foot curbs, built to contain the deluge of spring rains – exhausted, hungry, overburdened, overheated, overwhelmed by it all. At last I reach the school, ready to drop. A small boy is re-grouting the tiles of the courtyard. I attempt to explain who I am. He just stares. I stumble past, round a corner and see another person.

"*Hola.*" My voice creaks from cracked lips. "*Me llamo Marc.*"

The large man leaps up from the table, a wild beard exploding in all directions from his ruddy face, faded tattoos covering his bare arms. I soon learn he's Anna's just discovered brother, raised by different families, visiting from Oregon.

"Heyyy! Ya wanna beer?"

My gear slides from my shoulders and hands, sighing onto the floor. *Padre Perro* be praised.

"More than anything. Thanks."

Less than a week after this glorious welcome the country is at war. Timed to begin with the launch of NAFTA, Billy Clinton's gift to the neoliberal, neocolonial corporate powers, the Zapatistas struck on New Year's Day, taking the government completely by surprise. We wait for their arrival in Tapachula.

The first light comes, accompanied by the timpani of warfare. I jump from my cot and run to the courtyard, up the stone stairway to the second-floor classroom, from there to the roof. On all sides is a sea of flat roofs broken by water tanks like derelict freighters and courtyard walls with shards of broken glass embedded in the concrete. Beyond, the jungle climbs into mountains with peaks gauzed over in morning mist. Seemingly from everywhere come the sounds of a desperate battle. I search the horizon for the source of the din. Part of me is excited to witness this, more of me is scared shitless. But it turns out I am mistaken.

Zapatista Morning

Awakened at dawn
by gunfire & mortar shells
The war has arrived
& from rooftop's vantage
I search for explosions &
the clash of armies

Learning later
it's nothing but firecrackers
in a parade celebrating the feast day
of some damn saint or another
This cross-cursed country
is overrun with the damn fools

promising life or good harvests
wealth or health or luck or love
finding lost items or having safe travel
& most of all, solace from the thousand ills
brought to this land
by the same boats that brought the saints

& I just go back to bed
searching for a quiet parade
of dreams, free of guns & crosses
& the politics that peddle both

In the next few days, we learn who the Zapatistas are. From the surrounding towns, stories come in of people rushing from their homes to welcome the rebels. They prove to be not a foreign invasion, but a local indigenous force fighting to regain basic rights and living conditions long denied by a racist, corporatist government. We hear stories of entire villages being carpet-bombed because the government suspect the Zapatistas might be there, and if not, well, they're all just Indians anyway.

In a literal sense, the Zapatistas never come to Tapachula, but their presence and energy transform us all the same.

Antigovernment rallies fill the central plaza and the Mam *campesinos*, emboldened by the Zapatista successes, protest at the offices of the Subministry of Agrarian Reform and shut down the banks for weeks, demanding the return of privatized lands that had been held in common, and an end to unethical mortgage practices.

The government responds by filling the streets with soldiers patrolling in tanks and trucks. Heavily armed units go door to door each night, securing block after block – actions more likely designed to intimidate the locals than to find the insurgents. But the people continue in defiance, not only with their protests, but with their joy of life. The campesinos feed their children, cooking on sidewalk fires and sleeping on sheets of cardboard. The mariachis fill the night air with music. The expat poet nomads drink their Cuba libres and are happy they are unable to get paid due to the barricaded banks. Eventually, the banks cave, the campesinos go home in victory, the troops move on and the mariachis keep singing.

Xela

On the night she discovered the Mariachi Park
she knew she wouldn't be going home again
It was then she started using the name Xela
& stopped explaining herself to anyone

A row of tiny silver swords
running down his pantlegs, his guitar
telling tales of longing &
she tastes each note on her lips

Vagabond Song

> On the night she discovered the Mariachi Park
> she paused at my darkened doorway
> "The music," she said, "& the moon & everything
> & put me in your book," she said. "Just write:
> And then there was Xela."

We get word that an independent journalist from the States is coming to get the story from the locals and hopefully track down the elusive Subcomandante Marcos, the principal Zapatista spokesman, mistakenly identified as the leader of the egalitarian uprising. The reporter is coming in from Guatemala, we assume to avoid the attention of the Mexican government, and will be staying at our school. We're excited to welcome him, to play our part in getting the true story out to the rest of the world. I toy with the idea of accompanying him into the jungle to find Marcos. I don't know much about guns or military tactics, but I can chop wood and haul water for a few days, bring a bag of cornmeal, maybe in some small way pay my respects to the heroes who are standing up for the people.

Doña Anna takes a taxi to meet our guest at the bus stop. When she returns, I think she has picked up the wrong person. Our intrepid journalist turns out to be a pimply-cheeked trust-funder from Kalamazoo. The newspaper he's writing for is one his daddy put up the money for him to start. So far it has yet to publish an issue. But what it apparently has done is fund a tourist trip to Central America. The guy arrives lugging two immense Guatemalan-print duffel bags stuffed with trinkets, Mayan fabrics, decorative machetes, jewelry and woven hammocks: It's Columbus loading his ship all over again. I'm surprised the guy doesn't have a few *Indio* slaves stuck in his bags as well.

He sticks around for a few days asking the other Americans

at the school what they think is going on. We show him where the Socialist Party office is, thinking the guy there could give him some insight, maybe put him in touch with a good lead. But our trustaspondent doesn't speak any Spanish so he doesn't think he'd get anywhere with that. Instead he asks me to take him to Izapa, a small site of Mayan ruins nearby. He'd read about them in *Fodor's* (this *payaso* doesn't even know enough to use *Lonely Planet*). But I take him anyway. I'd wanted to see Izapa, and this way I can stick him with the bus fare.

Mayan Ruin

> On the two-peso combi to Talisman
> we ride, clustered and sweltering
> my knees dovetailed with those
> of an Indian woman nursing her child
> who returns my smile with a stone gaze
> & I feel like just another Cortés
>
> I'm dropped off in a pool of dust
> before the ruins of Izapa thinking
> she is the legacy of the Maya
> the history & destiny
> & these, after all,
> are just piles of rocks

We go through an unattended gate, passing a handful of cinderblock and scrap-wood huts. Dust-cloud chickens scatter at our approach. The remnants of small temples, pyramids and stelae rise from grassy plazas. Several of the features are protected by thatch-roofed canopies. The site is oriented toward the great volcano Tacaná. Turtles, frogs and serpents emerge from an ancient carver's chisel. The surrounding cacao trees shudder in the hot breeze. Almost at once the stones begin to speak to me. Ancient whisperings ... I fall into silence, listening. Unfortunately, our trusty trustaspondent has no ears.

Izapa

Tourists rarely come here

Compared to the grandeur of Tikál
or Copán or Chichén Itzá
this little field of stones,
few bigger than the nearby huts
of scrap wood & banana-leaf thatch,
is far from the trail
of must-see Mayan sites

Still, I find myself silenced
by a presence beyond definition
There is something here,
primal & profound
wise & mysterious
nameless

But then,
as I stand in their shadows
sinking under the weight
of the closest to the eternal
I may ever come,
the guy I'm here with
steps next to me,
snaps a picture without looking,
moves to the next structure,
snaps & moves on to the next

Before he gets to the fourth
I want nothing more
than to kill the little prick
& dump him in the brown water
of the ditch that carries life & poison

The Chicken Bus Highway, Part I

    to the homes beyond the low wooden fence
    holding a few skinny cows
    & a dog that hasn't quit barking
    since we got here

Somehow he survives and, fortunately for all of us, he soon returns to the States with his souvenirs and rolls of film and nothing at all to write about. In fact, his entire existence has been reduced to a brief scene as a clown in an unpublishable book by an unknown poet. Serves him right.

By the time he's home drinking wine coolers and regaling Tiffany and Kenneth with his daring adventures, we're making plans to climb Tacaná, a semi-active volcano (last eruption eight years previous) that straddles the border with Guatemala. At 13,320 feet, it's the second-highest peak in Central America, from which both the Pacific and Caribbean are visible. Cary, another American vagabond and my roommate at the school, has a tent and camp stove. I borrow a sleeping bag from Anna. Juan-Carlos, a local teenager, will be our guide. We rise early, pack some food and water and hike downtown to catch the chicken bus to Tuxtla Chico. From there, we wedge into a combi for the slow climb to Cacahoatán. We buy fruit from the Indian street vendors then hire a gypsy hack – the only kind of cab the town has – for a creeping, winding climb to the village of Unión Juárez – the closest we can get by vehicle.

Shouldering our packs, we begin the long hike: first a few miles of rough cobblestones on a narrow road rising into the forest, then a wagon path of hard-packed earth and ankle-breaking rocks. As we plod on, the Mam huts roofed with corrugated metal give way to ones thatched with banana leaves. The children at first run out to ask us for *dulces*, but as we go higher they hide in doorways, curiously yet fearfully watching our passing. We are getting into lands so remote that for any child under seven or eight, we are probably the first gringos they've ever seen. A final switchback brings us to a clearing with a scattering of stone-and-thatch houses and a two-room school building. School is in session and nobody's in sight. From here, a steep, writhing trail takes us into the clouds.

At a fork in the trail, we ask Juan-Carlos which way to take. He shrugs and says, "*No recuerdo.*" "I don't remember." This is repeated at each fork. Cary and I share a look, realizing that "guide" is perhaps not the right word for our companion. We peer up each branch of the trail and make a guess. As long as we are still going up, I figure we must be going the right way.

> Swallowed by forest &
> lost in cloud
> our feet trust the trail
> as our disoriented guide
> lags behind
>
> Swallowed by forest &
> lost in cloud
> the volcano watches
> our tottering progress
> in geologic silence

We were told before we left that there's a place called Los Papales where we can camp for the night before pushing to the summit the next morning. Of course, we will only get to this place if we guess correctly at each fork. We no longer bother to ask our guide. We're traveling on blind faith and dumb luck, and then Cary's knees force him to stop.

He drops his pack and slumps next to a boulder. Juan-Carlos

does the same, looking like he wishes he were back in Tapachula lounging in the shade and telling his friends how he knows Tacaná like the back of his hand. I sit as well and pass around a water bottle.

Cary is in much better shape than I am, but his knees are on fire. In training for this climb, we ran a few miles each night after the heat dissipated somewhat (it never really went far). But after the run, I would race up and down the stairs at the school twenty times without him – that difference has begun to show.

"I don't think I can go any farther," says Cary, passing the bottle to Juan-Carlos.

We rest for a while, and then I decide on a plan.

"I'll scout ahead and try to find Los Papales. If it's close enough, we can hobble there and camp, see how we feel in the morning."

I'm ignoring the fact that I don't know what Los Papales is or whether we are even on the right trail.

I leave my pack with the others, take another blast from the canteen and go. The trail rises more steeply, skirting a cliff that drops into cloud. One wrong step and I will be forever lost to the mountain's ravenous appetite. This isn't the kind of place where they recover bodies. It's just where I want to be.

> Lone pilgrim on Tacaná
> searching for Los Papales –
> either "the popes" or
> "the potato fields"
> – each equally unlikely
> but as the clouds thicken
> & hide the trail
> I begin to imagine
> a lost monastery of all the
> dead popes of history

Vagabond Song

> digging potatoes &
> pontificating to the birds
> who pass over unconcerned
> with the misguided mumblings below

I'm about to give up and turn back when I hear, through the mist, a rooster crowing. The popes must have kept the one Peter heard after his third denial, feeding it all these years on longevity-inducing potato skins. Perfectly logical – this has to be the right place.

I trot back down to Cary and Juan-Carlos and tell them we're close. Cary is reluctant, but I slip his pack on one shoulder and mine on the other and find him a walking stick. We stumble slowly up the trail.

Eventually we hear the rooster again, but it's impossible to accurately judge its distance. Visibility is down to a few feet and Cary is in severe pain. But if we stop here, we'd have to spend the night wedged between rocks at the edge of a cliff that seems to drop off into an endless void. If we didn't fall off, we'd die of exposure. On the other hand, if we push Cary's legs too hard we'll be faced with having to carry him all the way down – it would take days. The rooster crows again, sounding farther away.

Juan-Carlos and I help Cary to the ground. His face tells the story of his pain. We are in trouble. We're all exhausted, nerves are thin and I worry I brought them this much farther for nothing.

I walk a couple dozen yards on and search the haze. Just then the wind shifts and the cloud thins slightly. Through the milky gauze, I can just make out the ghost outline of a building, then another. I run forward, making out a small farm clinging to the side of the mountain. Chickens roam the rocky ground between a thatched hut and a loose grouping of sheds. A man appears at the doorway.

"¡*Hola!*" I call.

"¡*Buenas!*" the man answers, waving.

"¿*Es esto Los Papales?*"

"*Si, si. Los Papales. ¡Bienvenidos!*"

I drag my companions the final distance. *El Papa* shows us a thatched hut we can sleep in. The ground is less rocky and the slat-board walls will keep the winds from slipping through the thin fabric of our tent – or at least they will help. At this altitude we're in for a cold night, regardless. I build a fire, set up the tent inside the hut and join Cary and Juan-Carlos around the fire for a dinner of soup and tortillas.

> Corn soup & tortillas
> Fitting reward for a day of struggle
> as the fire burns low
>
> The comfort of exhaustion
> A singing sky of thatched leaves
>
> Huddled sleeping bags
> Larvae traversing the night
> in butterfly dreams

The frigid air of morning forces me out of bed to rekindle the fire. Stepping out into the predawn light is stunning. The clouds have completely cleared, revealing the mountains and forest in full splendor. The world is tinged with a copper glow. The forest, falling away all around, is glazed in a bright patina. A copper calf bounds over to me curiously. Copper chickens strut among the glowing rocks, scratching for insects.

With a charred stick, I scrape last night's coals into a nest, add a handful of twigs and, cheek to the ground, blow long, steady breaths. The white ash falls away and a small red glow responds to my resuscitation. Soon a flame leaps and grabs the twigs. I add small sticks and keep blowing. The fire has its resurrection at the same moment as the sun. That fire of all fires breaks free of the final grip of horizon and blazes wild. The volcano, whose mouth is still several hours up the trail, considers following suit, but decides to wait another year, or decade, or century – it's all the blink of a rooster's eye in Earth-time.

> Rooster holds
> the fire of the sun
> in its throat &
> beneath its terrible
> dinosauric feet
> can feel the breathing
> of the sleeping volcano
> knowing in its Cretaceous heart
> the moment is coming
> when this copper world
> will turn to gold

Cary joins me at the fire as I'm propping a stick between rocks to hang a pot of water. When the water begins to boil, I add handfuls of oatmeal, raisins and slices of apple.

"How're the knees?"

"Better. Some."

"You think we can keep going?"

Cary watches the dancing flames, reluctant to admit what we both know. But a good traveler knows when to back off.

"No," he says.

I can tell he's upset about preventing us from summiting. We've come a long way and it's not every day that you get to stare into the maw of a volcano and enjoy the view of two oceans. But it also isn't every day that you get to share campfire oatmeal with a good friend while a newborn sun paints the forest in amber.

I stir the coals, stir the oatmeal, and smile.

"The point of the journey is not to arrive," I say.

"Who's that?" asks Cary. "Lao Tzu?"

"Close," I say. "Neil Peart."

We're still laughing when Juan-Carlos joins us at the fire. He's ragged and beaten, cold and despondent, but his entire face smiles when we tell him we're not going any higher.

On the way down I walk point, letting gravity dictate the pace. The going is easy, spirits are high. Suddenly a subconscious, primordial alarm goes off and I freeze in my tracks, raising a hand to stop the others. A moment later, I see why.

Directly on the path before us, a large snake suns itself in the open space of our trail. It's a *gushnayera*, the venomous palm-pit viper. With luck on your side, probably not deadly. However, getting down the mountain with one of us racked with pain, swelling, nausea and bleeding that won't coagulate would be dire. If something deeper than my human brain hadn't stopped me, one of us would have stepped right on it, ensuring a bite.

The snake flicks its tongue, tasting our essence. A ripple of emerald light cascades along its slender body as scales arpeggiate from head to tail. It slides off the trail and into a hollow stump. We edge past slowly, with quiet respect.

> Louder: the music of the trees.
> Sweeter: the aroma-voices of the mountain.
> Brighter: the sunlight on each rock.
> These are the gifts of a venomous snake
> safely passed.

Vagabond Song

We arrive at the cluster of houses and the school we passed on the way up. The children are now on recess, swarming the schoolyard, kicking a flat soccer ball and playing a mysterious game that could be a distant relative of hopscotch. Spotting us, they cluster around excitedly. One runs into the school and returns with a basket of sweet bread, *pan dulce*, to share. Their teacher comes out and sits with us, telling us about this village, Chiquihuites, which means "place of the basket weavers."

This could be the name for the entire world of the Maya. The woven basket loaded with produce and balanced on the head of a Mayan woman is the iconic symbol of these people. (The same way a fat man with a gun, hamburger and flag is for the U.S.) Unfortunately, the art of weaving from natural materials is fading into history, like most traditional wisdom throughout the world.

About half of the baskets I see in the streets back in town are hand-woven from reeds and wooden splints. The rest are bright plastic bins bought at the markets. The plastic ones are more durable, they are waterproof, they can be bought in a second rather than taking hours to make. It wouldn't surprise me if the plastic version replaces the traditional basket within a decade. Progress marches proudly on.

The problem with this is twofold. When a traditional basket wears out, you toss it back into the forest. The plant fibers break down. Some become building materials for bird nests, some become food for insects, all of them eventually return to the earth to rebuild the soil and grow more plants to make more baskets. However, when a plastic tub breaks, you throw it out, and it sits there. Feeding nothing, of no use to the earth. Its chemicals leach into the groundwater, slowly poisoning the land and its inhabitants. Microplastics make their way to the sea and up the food

The Chicken Bus Highway, Part I

chain. So-called progress is little more than the creation of garbage, of waste; whereas in a traditional culture, by which I mean one in sync with natural cycles, nothing is waste. Everything remains part of a cycle. Progress or Western civilization or modern life is, at essence, that mode of existence that breaks out of the cycle and creates waste, and all waste is hazardous waste.

The second problem lies in the fact that no one in these villages can build that plastic tub. They must buy it. The more the convenience of the plastic erodes the knowledge of crafting the traditional basket, the more dependent the people become on a system of economic exploitation in which they must sell their labor and support the upward flow of wealth. They are drawn further away from freedom and further into wage slavery.

Thus a world that has broken with the natural way creeps in, destroying the health of the environment and the freedom of the people.

And, at that very moment, a third great illness of the schism from nature is marching up the hill toward Chiquihuites.

First one soldier breaks into the clearing. Then another. And another. They fan out, anxiously checking the houses and surrounding forest. Fingers hover fretfully over triggers. The children abandon their games, grow quiet and allow their teacher to gather them back into the school. We sit in the shade, chewing our pan dulce.

Within moments they have the town "secured," with soldiers stationed on rooftops, behind boulders and in a tight circle surrounding the three of us. The same alarms are going off in my body as with the snake, but more so. The snake was only dangerous if we were careless. Guns wielded in ideology are dangerous regardless of any degree of caution. My focus instantly narrows to the size of a rifle barrel. The forest and its music disappear. Only later do I notice I am breathing, sweating, cold. In the moment, I am only aware of the small black circles staring at me.

Their sergeant, or whatever he is, slips into the circle with a flurry of questions: "Who are you?" "Why are you here?" "Who else is with you?" "What have you seen?" All very simple to translate from Spanish to English, except when you are surrounded by a few dozen nervous guys holding rifles. I am struck, just as I was with Los Tigres who patrol the streets of Tapachula, by how young the soldiers are. But I guess all wars are fought by children.

Eventually we're able to explain that we teach at the English school back in the city, which seems to satisfy our interrogator. Then it's our turn. What are *they* doing here?

"*Solo un ejercicio de preparación.*"

Of course. I hide my smile with a bite of bread. It's always "just a training exercise." With live ammo. In an area rumored to be harboring Zapatistas. The look of fear on the child soldiers' faces tells the truth. If they had any courage, they'd tell this guy to fuck off and join the *revolución* themselves. Of course, if I had any courage, so would I.

      The children of Chiquihuites
      weave baskets by sharing *pan dulce* with strangers
      weave baskets by hiking miles of cloud forest
          to get to their two-room schoolhouse
      weave baskets by kicking a deflated ball
          across the village plaza

      The child soldiers come to Chiquihuites
      & unweave all the baskets
          in an instant

The Chicken Bus Highway, Part I

Back in the city, the war fades into the background. It's as Doña Anna said: "We just go on with our lives."

There are classes to teach, days spent at Playa Linda – eating the freshest shrimp I've ever had and toying with the riptide that claims a life every few years. And there are nights – long, wild, hazy nights at the bars – dancing to Bob Marley and the Gipsy Kings, though mostly it's bad pop swill from *el Norte*. We order Cuba libres and the bartender brings us a fifth of rum, a two-liter of Coke and a bucket of ice. We mix our own drinks – far too strong – and whenever supplies get low, replacements magically appear. The friends I come with eventually all leave and I find myself drinking with a table full of strangers, none of whom speaks any English. But my Spanish gets better with each drink. The bar stays open as long as we keep buying, or rather, *they* keep buying – my twenty-peso-per-week stipend only buys a couple cervezas or an occasional snack at Prontos or Viva Pizza. Eventually dawn comes and we pile into someone's car and head to a restaurant owned by one of these stranger-friends. He unlocks the door and cooks for us. Then I'm back in a car being driven through the waking streets, wondering how to explain where I live. An unnecessary worry – there are only a handful of gringos in town. *Everybody* knows where we live. The car pulls up in front of the school and I tumble out with a slurry of *"gracias"* and *"hasta luego."* Children pass in their uniforms on their way to the public school. Some of them, after their regular studies, come to our school for English lessons. These smile and call out.

"¡*Hola maestro!*"

I manage a wave and what I hope sounds like a friendly and somewhat professional growl, then stumble through the door toward my waiting cot.

Vagabond Song

    Two hours later, I haul my carcass up, grab a cup of tea and go to my Spanish lesson.

> My tutor conjugates
> & my early morning mind
> floating in a lake of *té de manzanilla*
> & the shoals of dreams
> designates meaning
> where none should be
>
> "*El nada en nada*," I say,
> "He swims in nothing."
>
> Fate, Struggle, God, Meaning, Everything
> dissolves into the lake's mist,
> the steam rising from a chipped cup
>
> "But you can't swim in nothing, *vato*,"
> says my teacher
>
> "Of course you can," I say,
> "It's poetry."

interludio

Señor Miscellaneous Jones
tiene tres cosas muy misteriosas y mágicas:
Una es el sombrero de San Juan Bautista
manchado con la sangre del rio
y otra es el pan hecho de la flor de arena
en el estadio del tiempo
Pero la tercera no tiene palabras
sólo color
y el color no es blanco
no es negro, ni nada en medio

The Chicken Bus Highway, Part II
sixth movement

El nada en nada on the chicken bus highway with a blue bandana piratewise over my head and eyes on the dancing horizon. All hands on deck. All decks are stacked. Land ho! and away we go.

At Cuidad Hidalgo we take a bike taxi up the long hill to the border crossing, singing '70s television theme songs. We walk across the bridge, get our passports stamped, and board a *gallinera* to Antigua. We have two weeks off for *Semana Santa*, Holy Week. Or in our case, weeks. Or months, decades, years.

"Everything is holy … the bum's as holy as the seraphim," sings Ginsberg.

I've scrounged together a few pesos from giving private English lessons to the spoiled, teenaged trophy wife of a coffee baron back in town. Cary and I are eager for the road. We'll get as far as we can.

On a former school bus from the States, repainted and packed five to a seat with the aisle filled SRO as well, we roll into Antigua,

Vagabond Song

Guatemala – the old capital before the government had enough of the earthquakes and moved to Guatemala City. We find a cheap *hospedaje* and stash our packs. Wandering the streets, we come to the remains of a cathedral. The façade stands before a field of earthquake rubble. Through its open doorway we can see a nearby volcano instead of the altar. It's a symbol for something, but it seems like a cliché. We turn away and go look for a drink.

At the Rainbow Bar and Reading Room the *cervezas Gallos* are cold, the energy of expats, vagabonds and backpack-bhikkhus is wild and flowing strong. It takes four or five bottles to wash the bus ride from my mouth. Among the bathroom graffiti someone has written: "What is it with you Canadians always having a Canadian flag on your backpack?" And another has answered: "Not to be rude, but the truth is, we do it so people won't think we're American."

Another result of the generations of our banana republic policies. I wonder where I can find a maple leaf patch. Or better, a black flag of No Country. No government, no ethnocentric bias, no lie of exceptionalism – just forests, mountains, rivers, lakes, seas and the dancing, dusty roads that connect them. All patriotism is fascism. I'll opt for matriotism instead.

One last bottle of Gallo, then off to a poet's dreams in the hard bed of the hospedaje. The next day will be the Palm Sunday Procession, reenacting the best welcome a weary traveler ever received. Of course, as with most Zen-hobo, Vagabond Angel, peacenik-commie, hippie lunatics, the welcome was short-lived.

In the morning, during a *desayuno típico* – eggs, black beans, corn tortillas, fried plantain drizzled with thick cream, and coffee – we watch the preparations. Dozens of people working for hours to create the trail for Jesus to walk: brightly colored mosaics of flowers and grasses, intricate and stunning. Also, geometric and floral designs rendered in sawdust dyed in bright hues. Block after block, seemingly covering the whole city. And then, hundreds of purple-robed believers filling the air with frankincense. Massive wooden altars, ornately carved, needing forty men to carry them. Jesus barely visible through the thick fog of incense.

It's a wondrous display, but I'll never understand how those peoples and cultures most attacked and damaged by the invading Christian forces have come to embrace this foreign religion with such vehemence.

It's the same story everywhere. Christianity has been wielded as a weapon to justify slavery: black skin was considered the mark of Cain and the African races were thought to be soulless agents of the Devil, and therefore had to be broken, whipped into submission. Yet today, the pervasiveness of this dominator religion among American blacks is almost complete. In Central America, the *conquistadores* used the weapon of religion to justify genocide, butchery, rape, infanticide and the most gruesome tortures imaginable. Today, finding a non-Catholic descendant of the Indigenous people is next to impossible. How can people so brutalized come to so strongly embrace the tool of their brutalization?

Of course, the Europeans who came to the Americas wielding this hideous weapon were descendants of the "pagan" peoples who were brutalized and subjugated by the "Holy" Roman Empire a couple of centuries earlier. Is this always the progression? Is this the natural method for the spread of this disease? Will the Southern Baptists someday colonize Planet X and whip the locals into submission with a Bible and a cross?

I can only hope the cancer of religion has run its course, and the Taliban and the Tea Party represent the last violent throes – its death rattle – and that the body of humanity will soon be free of this scourge.

Religion (*Chordeiles Minor*)

Nighthawk throws
its single song
across the darkening sky

Bell of a nearby church
begins to measure out
the remaining hours of the day

The bird falls silent –
listening … or not …
   – then returns

These opposites are noted
by a slightly aging man
on his back porch

The pure voice of that darting
wide-mouthed bird
catching insects on the wing

& the frail clanging
of two thousand years' worth
of dogma & doggerel

The man considers going inside
Decides to stay as the bell fades
& the bird returns

    Yet the ringing church bell holds beauty, as does the aroma of this incense, as do the mosaics of flowers being trampled by sandaled feet. And if it weren't for those former slaves of the American South finding Jesus, we wouldn't have gospel-soul music, and that would be a truly tragic loss.

Self-contradiction is the beginning of honesty. *Wade in the water, children. Dog's agonna trouble the water.*

Another morning of *huevos, frijoles negros, platanos fritos y tortillas* then off on the next chicken bus to Guatemala City to transfer to a main bus line (luxury travel with only three to a seat) – onward to El Salvador.

Enter Cindy Pilgrim, *vagabonda de* Idaho. Sharing a seat with Cary, one ahead of mine, passing road stories around like a bottle. By the time we get to San Salvador, we've decided to join forces for the night. The bus will continue on in the morning, with Cindy Pilgrim bound for Nicaragua. We'll head north into Honduras. But for now, the three of us wander off to find the WORSTHOTELINCENTRALAMERICA.

Granted, there's a lot of competition for this distinction. There are bad hotels. Seedy hotels. Run-down, ugly, blight-stricken hotels. There are grimy, gritty, grungy, gruesome hotels. There are disgusting, desolate, decadent, dingy, dilapidated, despicable, delirious, detrimental-to-your-health hotels. There are heinous, horrendous, horrible, hideous, hellish, honest-to-Dog-you-wouldn't-send-your-worst-enemy-to hotels. There's the Devil's Dormitory, Satan's Sleep, Lucifer's Lounge, Antichrist's Attic and Beelzebub's Bed and Breakfast, but there is only one WORSTHOTELINCENTALAMERICA, and we found it.

It must have been a former warehouse, maybe for exhaust manifolds or broken doll heads, but it may also have served time as a slaughterhouse, a drug house, a whorehouse and a flophouse. In fact, it may still be all of those. The door opens into a cavern where a few naked light bulbs are losing their battle with the darkness. The reception desk is behind a barred window like an

Vagabond Song

eastside liquor store. We slide a few *colónes* under the bars and a figure lost in shadow slides back a small key attached to a large block of wood. A skeletal finger points to a dank stairwell.

"*Cuartos. Arriba.*"

The second floor, where the "rooms" are, is an open space with a line of small windows on one wall. Through the grime-encrusted glass, I watch a cluster of chickens on connecting rooftops peck through rotting garbage tossed from other windows, giving urban farming a whole new meaning. Opposite the chicken-viewing windows are the "rooms." "Rooms" must forever be in quotation marks, and even then the word's a stretch. Panels of particleboard have been attached to vertical two-by-fours. Since the panels are eight feet and the ceiling is ten, there is a one-foot gap above and below the "walls" of the "rooms." Inside, through a "door" of particleboard, is the "bed," a wooden cot with a communion-wafer-thin mattress – a wafer that has been chewed on and spat out by an ornery old Mother Superior who had finally had enough of the Church and realized she had wasted her entire life.

In the corner opposite the stairwell is a single-stall "bathroom" that hasn't enjoyed running water for years, which doesn't stop legions of guests from using it anyway. Just to walk past its one-hinged door is to court a host of pernicious diseases that would leave one nastily maimed or, if lucky, dead.

Drinks are definitely needed if we are to survive the night. Whiskey. Heroic, monumental amounts of whiskey.

> San Salvador cantina
> whiskey, whiskey, whiskey & Cindy Pilgrim
> overflowing bliss until
> she slams my thumb
> in the taxi door

The Chicken Bus Highway, Part II

    & I'm reminded
    of all the miles
    I haven't traveled

    A misread invitation
    leaves me with a quarter of a cot,
    a throbbing thumb and throbbing head
    Hours later, crossing the border,
    I'll catch my error &
    laugh at myself for what
    could have been

In the morning, Cary and I board the rock-n-roll chicken bus, decked out in psychedelic colors, packed to the gills with beautiful, sweating humanity and the obligatory shrine to Mother Mary built into the upper corner next to the door. When this was a simple yellow school bus, the spot probably held a fire extinguisher. What a waste of space – let the Virgin put out all your fires!

The driver is a madman, barreling around narrow mountain curves that lack even a token guardrail between us and a long date with Mary's boyfriend. He dances in his seat to the '60s tunes blasting from trembling speakers, oblivious to the flirting cliff, and – because none of that is quite dangerous enough – he's teaching his twelve-year-old son how to drive by standing up and letting the kid slide into the seat to take the wheel. They switch back and forth a half dozen times before we get to the Honduran border.

On the Road to Copán

    In a cheap room
    in Antigua Ocotepeque
    a scorpion from under the bed

Vagabond Song

    walks between my bare feet

    On a bus packed like a cattle car
    a Mayan girl frets
    over her dying, dehydrated
    chicken

    The sun is obliterating
        relentless
            indifferent

    I imagine pouring water
    for the chicken, I
    save it,
    save the girl,
    save her family
    save the Indigenous poor everywhere

    A thick-soled sandal
    is within reach,
    brings all my fear and ignorance
    slamming down
    on the scorpion
    like a missionary

    The sun carries a U.S. passport
    wrapped in a rosary
    I take a drink of water
    close my eyes

    We grab a hospedaje in Copán, stash our packs and make the rounds. Cobblestone streets with nearly as many horses as cars wind past markets and homes. Most of the town's architecture is colonial, with red tile roofs and arched doorways. At a sidewalk café, we order bottles of the national beer, *Salva Vida* – "life saver," an apt name after a sweltering bus ride. We buy a bag of sweet bread at a bakery and church bells to lead us to the central plaza.

Chalk Gods

A boy sells trinkets
in the park in Copán
drops a small chalk carving
of a Mayan god
he wants us to buy

The god shatters at our feet
as they all do

He can't return home
empty-handed
so we give up our bag
of *pan dulce*
for his mother

If we only had bread
in place of our gods
we would see that
Earth *is* Heaven &
there's no need for salvation

The children of the park gather
as we show them how
to use the pieces of broken chalk
to draw on the sidewalk

I draw a house
& they draw the sun & moon
I draw a rocket
& they draw a horse & tree
Learning, I draw a bird
& they surround it with flowers

They draw until the chalk god
disappears in their hands

Rented horses take us into the mountains. Our ten-year-old

Vagabond Song

guide rides with me, revealing ruins of ancient villages beneath the verdant tangle of jungle. He points out a boulder carved into a frog that once served as a gate marker identifying the place. "Welcome to Frogtown. Population 0." The trail is narrow, rocky and steep. If my horse stumbles, we'll fall off a cliff into bone-shattering rock. The view is worth the risk. The rolling canopy rides the rise and fall of the land, alive with the sounds of macaws, trogons and groove-billed anis. A troop of spider monkeys ripples through, mostly only visible as a trail of shaking branches.

Coming to a river, *el Rio Copán*, we meet a tobacco farmer who gives us fresh leaves from the rafters of his drying shed. That night, back at the hospedaje, we roll the leaves into tight cylinders and smoke them on the porch. The flavor contains the sunlight on the mountain slopes, the quiet song of the river, the danger and thrill of that narrow trail, the crystalline depth of the horses' eyes, the laughter of our child guide, the farmer's smile, *el silencio de la selva*. It is the best smoke I've ever had.

At *las Ruinas de Copán*, the ceiba trees – the Mayan Yggdrasil – tower over the temples, which are returning to the soil as I watch. The architecture is stunning, the scale arresting, but this is what I have to say: Any empire built on slave labor not only deserves to fall, but *will* fall. That's the unavoidable truth of all great "civilizations" ruled by leeching priests and kings. Empires fall. Ask Rome. Ask Egypt. In 50 or 100 years, ask the USA. I fill up two rolls of film, awed by what I see, but at the same time thinking I could be looking at the Washington Monument, Mt. Rushmore, the Empire State Building. This is where those braggadocios are heading. *The lone and level sands stretch far away.*

I hand my camera to Cary so he can snap a picture of me at the base of a gigantic, twisting tree growing from the top of some forgotten tyrant's lair. For all his power and glory, all his dreams of immortality, a tiny seed broke into his cold skull and grew. No matter what man builds in a desperate and vainglorious attempt to conquer the egalitarian anarchy of the Earth, nature wins in the end. The natural democracy of all living things prevails over man's petty tyrannies.

> The gods & kings
> are made of chalk
> the children are in need of neither
>
> Temple, palace & corporate HQ
> march toward their identical end –
> compost for the trees that will always return

Bus after bus leaves San Pedro Sula, packed beyond reason with families. It's Easter Sunday and apparently the entire country goes to the beach at Puerto Cortés (the Killer). We are going there to catch the boat to Belize. Each hour, a bus pulls into the dirt lot and is instantly swarmed by a desperate mob fighting to get on. After the third hour of politely waiting for "our turn," we realize the only way to get on the bus is to use the local method. Following the next arrival, we push and shove and squeeze and slide and elbow and shoulder and jockey and block and grunt and hiss and slither and finally make it on board. The overloaded bus groans out of the station, leaving a knotted mass of disappointment in its wake. We can't move or breathe. I'd like to take a drink from my water bottle, but the crush of bodies makes it impossible to even move my arm. And yet, everyone seems perfectly content. Just another Sunday ride to a day at the beach. Happy Easter.

We arrive and pour like pine sap from the bus. But at the dock we find out that the cost for the trip to Belize is ten times higher than we thought. An impossible scenario, so instead we have a couple cervezas and tortillas wrapped around a bit of cheese and a stalk of green onion, and wait for the next bus. The ride back is almost empty – only four to a seat.

> Why do Cortés & Columbus
> have cities named after them
> but Hitler & Himmler do not?
> Simple: Their team won.

Our new plan is to go to Puerto Barrios, back into Guatemala, and catch a boat there to Livingston, a rasta beach town on *la Bahía de Amatique*, surrounded by jungle and accessible only by water.

The bus to the port doesn't leave until midnight so Cary and I stash our packs at the station and head to the central plaza to wait. The woman at the bus station tells us not to be in the park after sunset, to take a cab, and not to walk the streets after dark, as if the city were overrun with vampires every night. Her concern borders on the hysterical, so we promise her we'll get off the streets in time and will make it safely back to her.

At the plaza, hundreds of people lounge in the shade. Vendors sell fresh produce, bootleg cassettes and plastic junk from Chinese sweatshops. At folding tables under tarps, old men play the card game *brisca* or dominoes surrounded by crowds of spectators. We figure it's some city tournament and watch for a while. The crowds watch every play intently, but don't seem invested in any particular player. It's more like they're watching a fascinating documentary on game playing.

To pass the time, we buy a deck of cards and find a quiet spot to play a few hands of cassino. Before long a few people gather

The Chicken Bus Highway, Part II

to watch, then more. By the third hand, a crowd of two or three dozen surrounds us. We try to explain that we're not part of the tournament; we're just passing time. One guy quickly becomes the spokesman for our audience by merit of having once lived in Chicago. He explains that there is no tournament.

"Then why are they watching us?"

"They're bored," says Chicago. "They have no money to do anything else."

Well then, I think, let's entertain them! I start performing card tricks taught to me by my grandfather and a former roommate who studied as a magician. Cary translates my patter into better Spanish than I'm capable of. I do the "Four Brothers," the "Ambitious Card," the "Nine Card Deal" – I hit them with double lifts and Herrmann passes and the Hindu shuffle. The crowd is spellbound. When I run out of tricks, we move on to tongue-twisters and jokes. For the next hour we bring vaudeville to Honduras, our crowd growing all the time.

But then there's a sudden change in the air. The crowd evaporates. Chicago says he has to go, and we should too. Dusk has crept into the sky and the park is nearly empty, save for several clots of shadowy figures slowly closing in from all sides.

Vampires.

They're after money rather than blood. Of course, if our blood happens to get in the way, *no es importante*.

We pack up our cards and beeline for the brightly lit hotel across the street. Another minute out there would have been the end of us. We decide to heed the advice of the bus clerk and stay inside, then cab it back to the station. In the bar, we grab a table by the window and watch the slow parade of vampires searching out the night's prey. Junkies needing pocket change for their next fix and more than willing to slit a throat to get it. Just another reality of condensing poverty into a large city. Just more fallout from the bombs of capitalism, colonialism and trickledown desperation.

Darkness seals the sky. The moon's away on business. We nurse Cuba libres, waiting for midnight. The vampires will own the streets until dawn. When our cab comes, we dart from the door, ignoring a voice that calls from the shadows. Just before sliding into the car, I look up.

> The night's only star –
> a moth caught in the streetlight
> Still, I make my wish

In Puerto Barrios, the Chiquita Banana port is guarded by tall concrete walls topped with barbed wire. Soldiers of a private militia armed with automatic rifles and shotguns roam the compound and are posted in guard towers. All this for bananas? It would be a confusing sight without a basic history lesson of Central and South America. A cursory glance at the legacy of American intervention makes it clear.

The method is simple. The U.S. military trains handpicked sociopaths in the latest methods of autocratic terrorism and torture at the School of the Assassins at Fort Benning in Georgia. The CIA orchestrates a coup, putting their newly graduated puppet in charge. The puppet is free to rape, pillage, murder and "disappear" his people, just as long as he keeps his prime directive in mind: the resources of his country must be channeled into the coffers of key U.S. corporations. Here that has primarily meant United Fruit. If the people organize cooperative farms in order to earn a living wage or to free themselves of the illnesses and birth defects associated with the pesticide rain they are routinely doused with, United Fruit makes a phone call to its puppet who, with the full support of the U.S. government and corporate media, declares the operation a communist uprising and sends in the troops. If, in a bizarre fluke of negligence, democracy happens and the people elect a leader they choose rather than one chosen by the corporations, the U.S. spares no expense in either covertly or openly supporting the overthrow of the "regime" by the "freedom fighters" until a puppet who won't question his strings can be brought back to power.

It happened here in 1954. Haiti in 1915. Bolivia in 1971. Chile in 1973. Brazil in 1964. Nicaragua for several long decades. The list goes on.

I snap a furtive picture of a uniformed guard brandishing a shotgun. The bananas are safe today, while vendors at the market have only blackening rejects to sell. The café only has bags of instant coffee. Chiquita's bullets are all top shelf.

The boat to Livingston is a rusting barge with rows of wooden benches splintering in the brutal sun and saltwater spray. We chug along the coastline of Amatique Bay, past the impenetrable jungle. North of us the Caribbean spills out, holding Cuba and its surprisingly close neighbor, Florida. I-75 begins there. Five states later, the same highway passes by my old hometown. This is the closest I've been to home in months. But then again, it's a tourist who is far from home. The traveler is always there.

Back in Copán, at the gateway to the ruins, I felt the difference between these two, or rather, the difference in the effect they have on locals. The traveler gives off a vibe of belonging in a place; a tourist gives off a vibe of invading it. People feel and respond to the difference. While waiting to enter the ruins, I was approached

Vagabond Song

by a young Mayan girl selling necklaces of brightly dyed beans.
"*Tu compra,*" she said. "*Buen precio solo para ti.*"
It's always a "good price, just for you."
"*¿Cuantos?*"
"*Tres por cinco lempiras.*"
Three for five. The going rate for joints back in the States. But in this case, it's about seventy cents. Like Jack, I bought the beans. Then she turned to the loud, pushy, obviously American tourist nearby.
"You buy? Good price, only for you," she says, using English this time.
"How much?"
"Twenty lempiras, each."
The tourist sorted through the strands, criticizing their lack of refinement, commenting on how cheap they were, and bought five. But then the girl turned back to me and smiled. I was included in her heist. On the same team.
It's good to be home.
The ferry bounces against a row of old tires tied to a wooden pier. Lines are thrown and secured, and we disembark in Livingston. Small fishing boats bob alongside rippled docks, young boys sort out tangled nets, elders laze in the shade of thatched cabanas. We stash our gear in a cheap room and head to the beach.
Our island is waiting for us fifty yards from shore. Tanned rock with a smattering of green and brown grasses and a single stunted palm tree quivering in the Caribbean breeze. We wade out and claim it in the name of the broken crown of the anti-king. Another *U-topos*, population: one tree and two joy-crazy nomads.
The afternoon drifts by like a boat on the horizon with an opium-addled captain. A figure on the beach waves, then begins

The Chicken Bus Highway, Part II

swimming out to our island. Soon he's climbing up beside us, the water and sun glistening on his obsidian skin, which is broken only by a red Speedo. His African heritage appears to dominate his Arawak side. He, like most of the people of Livingston, is Garifuna – descendants of Ibibio people from what is now Nigeria. Their ship, bound for the slave markets of the French West Indies, went down and the survivors made it to the island of Bequia. They intermarried with the local native population and formed a distinct culture. The older generation here speaks only Garifuna, the younger ones add Spanish, French and passable English. In the case of our new friend, all at once.

"*Allo! ¿Que onda?* I am Kissinger, de diplomat, mon. Anyting you need, I git it for ya, mon. *¿Mota?* Smoke? One pound for *dix dólares*."

I must have heard him wrong. The wild jumping from language to language makes me feel like I'm in a pinball machine. There is no way a pound of weed is only $10. Besides, what the hell would I do with that much? I'd get busted at the border for sure, and would spend the next twenty years rotting in some Central American prison. My parents would spend their life savings trying to get me released. The strain would be too much – their marriage would crumble, my dad would drop from a heart attack, my mom would move down here fighting for me until she was completely broke and broken. She'd end up wandering the streets of Guatemala City like a *madre de los desaparecidos*. Some Hollywood jerk would make the whole thing into a movie and get rich off it. At the end of the film, the screen would read: "Marc now lives in a halfway house in Detroit. He still suffers from frequent nightmares of rabid spider monkeys wearing Pat Boone masks."

"*¿Que nesecitas*, mon? Anyting you need. I am de diplomat. I am Kissinger. I git it for you."

"*Solo quiero una poca mota*," I try to explain. "Just a little."

"*Si, una poca.* Just one pound. You come wit me. I cook you *comida. Muy sabrosa. Très* good. We go to my house. I make good food for you. I am Kissinger, de diplomat."

The man is clearly crazy, somewhere between drugged-out and full-blown whackadoo, but a home-cooked meal sounds great and if he's selling elbows of ganga for ten bucks, I can probably have a nice smoke for free and not have to spend the rest of my life in a jail cell.

"Okay, Kissinger, *vamanos*. Lead on, *Monsieur* Diplomat."

We swim to shore and Kissinger leads us immediately to the nearest bar. He orders three beers and starts dancing to the mariachi on the radio. The bartender brings the bottles and we pay. This is repeated twice more on the way to Kissinger's house for our home-cooked meal. At each bar we pass, Kissinger drags us in, orders the drinks and has us pay. He never stops dancing to whatever music is playing. We soon realize he has no money, or pot, or probably food. We also notice how unenthusiastic each bartender is to see "de diplomat." Finally we have to explain that we aren't buying any more beer – "*No mas cerveza. ¡Nada, nada, nada!*" – so Kissinger will give up on the bars and take us to his home.

We follow him down a sandy path into a jumble of shacks made of bamboo staves and covered in corrugated metal or palm leaves. He brings us to his home – a single room with a metal cot covered only with a burlap bag, no mattress or blanket. On a shelf is a candle, a tin cup and some shells. And that's it. No other furniture. No clothes. *Nada*. Back outside, he brings us before an ancient matriarch bent into an old wooden chair. He introduces her as his grandmother who speaks only Garifuna. We talk briefly, with Kissinger translating, and would love to have talked more, but now Kissinger wants to take us to the market to buy food for our dinner. We know that means more bars, more free drinks from the gullible gringos. We have to lose de diplomat before we're broke – and just as drunk as he.

We make an excuse to go back to our hotel, but he insists on following us. Fortunately, the desk clerk knows him and won't let him inside. We tell him we'll be back soon, and then go to our room and wait. Once the coast is clear, we head out to find a restaurant. We spot Kissinger later that night, but he's far too drunk to recognize us.

The night ends with a couple of Gallo beers at the water's edge behind our hotel. A group of kids are taking turns climbing into a broken baby stroller that they're all too big for and having the others push them into the water. Their laughter is full of some innocent freedom that I'm not used to. It is somehow richer and wilder than the laughter of American children. What is it that those who have nothing have that those who have so much lack?

Non qui parum habet, sed qui plus cupit, pauper est. "It is not he who has little, but he who craves more, who is poor." Perhaps Seneca once drank a Gallo in the moonlight listening to the laughter of rich poor children.

We go to bed with that sound still dancing in our ears and are up before light to catch the early boat back to Puerto Barrios.

On Amatique, Missing Dawn

>The waves still hum
>with the mist of the night's song
>as two dozen strangers
>make the first run of the day

Vagabond Song

from Livingston back to Puerto Barrios

I fold my arms inside my T-shirt
try to daydream away the biting predawn cold

Across the black ribbons of the curving sea
across Cuba & Boca Chica Key
across the golf courses
    & plastic surgery clinics of Florida
across the slave quarters of Georgia
across the trailer parks & junkyards of Kentucky
across the Great Smokies & Blue Ridge
across Newark, Ohio where my ancestor
    Samuel Parr built the first house
    & is buried under a stone patinaed with lichen
across the poisoned rivers & silent auto plants
    of southeast Michigan
across the sugar beet fields & marshes
    of the Saginaw Valley
across the streets of Bay City
    named for dead presidents
across a yard of dandelion & a rusting bicycle
through a dog-scratched door
    into a house of skeleton keys
up a wide stair, down a long hall
is a room where a young boy once sat
staring out a window
to a world that, beyond imagination, held this boat

On the tattered horizon
is a gathering of light
& I lean forward on this bench
expecting at any moment
my first ocean-view sunrise

The boat slaps each wave like a lullaby
& I'm so cold & so tired
& still the sun is buried
in the night-grave of the Caribbean …

> Perhaps it's the wash of warmth on my face
> or the tease of light on my eyelids
> that wakes me suddenly to find
> a blue sky over blue sea
> & the quick pain of another
> missed sunrise

Sololá is rebel-controlled territory and as the bus climbs to its ridgeline border, the tension builds proportionally. At a checkpoint, we are taken off the bus by soldiers. Some passengers are pulled aside for questioning. The rest of us are put on a different bus, as if crossing into a foreign country. On the hills above, more soldiers are perched behind sandbag bunkers, only their eyes and rifle barrels visible. Everyone is quiet and tense. On the new bus, there are fewer of us. I can't see where the missing ones have been taken, but as we begin the descent into the heart of the guerilla lands a collective sigh of relief passes through the bus. Soon everyone is talking and laughing. The driver tunes in a local station playing dance music, and smiles are easily come by.

The message is clear: the government is dangerous, unpredictable and violent, like an injured beast. The rebels are protection from that animal, at least here, at least for the time being.

At the village of Panajachel, dozing along the shore of Lake Atitlán, volcano-ringed and crystalline, we swing our packs over our shoulders and seek out the cheapest room.

"*¿Hay cuartos aquí?*"

"*Sí.*"

"*¿Hay agua caliente?*"

"*No, pero no es necesario.*"

"*Verdad.*" In этой heat, hot water is useless. We'll only want cold showers. But they do have rooms.

Vagabond Song

"¿*Cuantos?*"
"*Ocho.*"
Eight quetzales. Hell of a deal.
"*Bueno. Gracias. ¿Tiene usted cervezas aqui?*"
"*Sí, sí. ¡Muy frio!*"
A cot in a cinderblock hut for a buck fifty and cold beer on hand. My dream lodging. Beats any Holiday Inn on the planet. We settle in and splash cold water on our faces to revive ourselves from the stupor of bus travel, then head downtown to see what life wants to throw our way next.

Cantata for the Vagrants

I
All these bum writers
sitting in Central American *comedors* & sidewalk cafés,
downing cervezas & instant coffee
    (because all the real beans are sent north)
scribbling on notebooks, journals, napkins, menus
carving lines & bleeding words
pausing only to buy trinkets from
        the insistent Mayan children
           (woven bracelets & plastic beads,
                ceramic birds & colored beans)
    & to order another cup, another bottle,
    another spent peso or quetzal or coloné,
    another hour tossed into the hands
        of the mountain winds
wondering how long they can bask in obscurity
wondering where the next wheezing
        overloaded chicken bus will lead

It is these dusty, bright-eyed bums
that I call out to
as I sit in this dark comedor
in the Guatemalan highlands
with a cup of pale, gritty coffee

The Chicken Bus Highway, Part II

scribbling, scribbling, scribbling

Sharing a hammock, sharing the sun-stippled waters of Atitlán, we savor the slow passing of the day. Cary and I have hooked up with a German vagabond with hair and eyes the color of the ravens I once watched slicing the dawn sky above the spruces of the Lake Superior shoreline. The ticket clerk at the bus station back in Guat City told us we should take care of her: she's traveling alone and doesn't speak Spanish. We're happy to, though it seems unnecessary. She floats through the world, untouched, mysterious and calm. A swan in the predawn fog, too beautiful to capture or even touch. I can't remember her name, but it was something out of a Wagner opera.

A young Mayan girl comes along selling woven *camisas* in the traditional pattern of her village, San Pedro la Laguna, which lies across the lake from the more touristy Panajachel. We have no money to buy so instead she shares her bag of peanuts and joins us on the hammock. The sun continues its imperceptible ooze along the bark of the sky.

II
We gather at night
in the hippie bars that swirl
like tidal pools of guiltily spoken English –
the Grapevine, the Rainbow Room, the Circus Bar –
A guitarist plays worn-out covers of the Doors &
    Van Morrison
Miguel pops a hash cookie into my mouth
& I wash it down with a Gallo –
    the new Eucharist, but it's all the same to me
    I'll take salvation however it comes
The Costa Rican angel pushes his thick hair from
    dilated eyes
    his Californian disciple smiles like Kasapa

Vagabond Song

) it's happy hour here & the two-for-one Cuba libres
swim through my brain clarifying everything (

The ancient grandmother
slips in among the drinkers
selling necklaces & woven cloth
Later I see her slumped on the cobblestone road –
 a pile of rags & bones –
tipping a brown, unlabelled bottle
to a wan & waning moon

Miguel invites me back to his room – another cinderblock hut with a single cot and room for a backpack and nightstand. From the decorations and clutter, it looks like he's been living here for some time. There's no place to cook, so Miguel has perfected a recipe for hash no-bake cookies, which he shares like loaves and fishes. Others show up and a party erupts.

Miguel rolls a joint. An epic, volcanic, soon-to-be-legendary spliff. A jay to be reckoned with. We reckon. I become fluent in Spanish and French while my English becomes a bird at the window, threatening to fly off to the nearest ceiba tree. We speak only in poetry. Prose is for mortals – shopkeepers and logicians. By the time I leave, I have absolutely no idea where I am or how to find my room. I wander the narrow, dark streets remembering stories of strangers' knives and fearing the pathetic possibility of becoming nothing more than a statistic or a page 3, below-the-fold headline: "Tourist found dead, robbery suspected" though even the poorest of thieves would be sorely disappointed by the take: a few centavos and a bottle cap.

The Chicken Bus Highway, Part II

    III
Sun-gilt bamboo
draped in wood smoke
laundry spread out to dry
on grassy banks of brown rivers
naked children dancing in the shallows
Mother, grandmother, daughter,
holy crying prostitute,
lay your lost sons & lovers
on burning mattresses
cover us with mosquito nets
lest we lose the remains
of our song-laden blood

On the lake, fishermen in hand-hewn canoes. In the streets, vendors with bananas and tortillas still warm from stone ovens. In the hills, the protective silence of the rebellion. On the horizon, a ring of volcanoes saying, "Live this moment fully, wildly, joyously, for tomorrow or the day after could be your last." In the markets, the music of bartering and spinning coins. At the sidewalk café, the writer dancing with his pen.

    IV
Clustered in the concrete tomb/womb
assaulted by the light of a bare 100-watt bulb
minds lulled by the flypaper of our drunkenness
but our souls like the quetzal
fly to the jungle canopy
when green feathers are plucked from a plastic bag
rolled into a volcano
& ignited

) we are in the Moment & the Moment is always poetry (

speaking rapidly/rabidly in Spanishenglishfrench
allatonce, one beautiful beast with many mouths
the kid spilling mad verses learned from lizards

Vagabond Song

    & father cockroach
the nocturnal eyes of *La Oscura* flashing
within the aura of musk & fateful raps
on the door of my undoing
a drum & guitar add their voices
though I can't see who, if anyone, is playing –
we're all playing
playing Fill-in-the-Blank:

    … womb _____ tomb …

Later I wander the littered streets
hopeless(full)ly lost & stumbling
haunted by stories of American tourists
found dead – blood staining the corn leaves
or the intern's story of the cold-storage room
at the university
where hundreds of cadavers hung
by ice picks jabbed in their ears
& his recurring dream
that at night, in the blackness,
they would begin to sing, but,
deafened by the picks,
would never hear their song

Finally back at my two-dollar room
the illness comes
& I sink to the concrete floor
of a rotting outhouse
gasping, moaning, rolling my head
on its sunburnt stalk
& wait to be purified

    Crossing back into Mexico, you walk through a narrow gate where a button stands guard on a metal post. Above the button are two lights, one green and one red. Pushing the button makes one of the lights wake up: green and you're free to enter, red and you're taken away to be searched. Supposedly the result is random, but there are rumors that the guard in the booth can light whichever he chooses, based on the look of the button-pusher. If this is true, surely a longhaired, bearded, bandannaed, Jesus-sandaled, wild-eyed freak will get the red light. No big deal, unless the longhaired, bearded, bandannaed, Jesus-sandaled, wild-eyed freak just happens to have three joints, gifted to him by Miguel before leaving Panajachel, stuffed in his underwear. In that case, it becomes a very big deal.

But there is no turning back – there never is. I push the button and wait. Eons pass. The guard's glare penetrates my cortex and all my sins are revealed. A trickle of electricity inches along a thin wire, making its way to one of two lights. The whole world stops breathing.

Then the green light comes on and I walk on through. *¡Bienvenidos a casa, hermano!*

> V
> & it was somewhere in Honduras
> the dust swirling around our crawling bus,
> an obese cloud pulling itself by its fingertips
> over the edge of the mountains
> threatening the valley with rain
> I could feel the strain of the land
> the tension of rock & sky
>
> If the storm were fully upon us
> or the air did not carry its promise
> we might escape the clutch of gravity
> & join the old gods
> on the shoulders of the ceiba
> but the uncertainty, the wait,
> hold us fast to this road
> of scorpions & cinderblock huts

Vagabond Song

> Still, we are traveling on
> We are traveling on

Returning to Tapachula and the routine of classes, everything now feels intimately familiar: the orchid seller playing folk songs for children by whistling on a banana leaf held between his thumbs, the horse carts clopping amid belching buses and ramshackle taxis, the garbage man clanking his chimes of scrap metal from the top of his truck telling us to race our trash to the corner and throw it in, the one-legged peanut vendor who sings as he mixes the warm nuts with chili powder and lime juice, the mariachis in their park who serenade couples for two pesos a song. By being away, this place has become home.

The night before returning to the States, Cary and I go to Playa Linda with *mi amiga loca*, Nadia and another friend of hers. Nadia and I smoke one of Miguel's jays and stare out at the dark ocean. The moon is dropping toward its watery grave and its light casts a trail across the gently rolling sea. The crashing of the surf builds in my head until it pushes beyond hearing.

"*El sonido del mar es silencio,*" I say to the night, trying to write the coming poem on the black pages of the sky.

"*¿Mandé?*" asks Nadia. But I just continue.

"*La luz de la luna es un camino hacia lo infinito.*"

"*Estas loco.*"

"*Sí, muy loco.*"

"*Estas borracho.*"

"*Sí, muy borracho.*" I stand and address the sea. "*Los poetas siempre se emborrachan de la luna. Siempre.*"

The Chicken Bus Highway, Part II

El Sonido del Mar es Silencio

1
Somewhere between
an endless field of morning-closed wildflowers
& the bitterness of another rented room,
I stand waist-deep in the sea's embrace
allowing the riptide to drag me through the sand
into a mystery we can know but once

Listen:
The way the wind sometimes
catches a dead leaf
& transforms it in the space of a pulse beat
into a bird taking flight
is the kind of miracle one should live for –
I have been told
you must never watch
a bird fly past the horizon or it will take
some small part of your soul with it

But what is the soul
if not the sum
of the flights
of a thousand birds?

2
The sea at Puerto Madero
is warmer than tears
cats continually at the feet of Chiapas
is sister not to the rivers of jungle valleys
& coffee plantations
but to the patient volcanoes
like Tacaná, thunder & haze
of the Guatemalan border

We spent two days climbing
crossing the path of a death-offering snake

Vagabond Song

eating *pan dulce* with village children
& being questioned by the Mexican Army
on patrol, looking for Zapatistas

When they find them
let each soldier fall to his knees
& beg forgiveness for the last 500 years
Let them speak the names of the dead
Let their mouths be filled
    with the dust of the graves
Let this be true for every soldier, but more so,
for every priest of the Pentagon
every general of Wall Street
every tycoon of evangelism

Let it be true for you
& me

3
The sound of the sea contains everything
swells out of control if we try to listen
overwhelms our capacity to hear until
infinite sound
       becomes
              silence

El sonido del mar es silencio
500 years in a single wave
   Silencio
History rises & falls with a single tide
   Silencio
It was the children who gave us sweet bread –
      we had nothing
   Silencio
Always: Another bird with eyes of ocean
takes to the sky

caesura: **Symposia**

IN THE GORY OLD GREEK TRADITION, our gathering place for much talk and much drink. Poetry and music, philosophy and politics – cases of Grain Belt beer in place of the *kraters* of wine. Specifically, an unheated attic squat in a St. Paul apartment building where Francisco and I make a winter home and base for insurgent operations. We tack up blankets to create bedrooms, get used to sleeping in long johns and stocking caps and compose poems and songs that are all odes to Chaos.

Raiding the ten-cent veggie bin at the co-op, we make vats of soup that become stew then chili then goulash, and finally reheated and thickened to make veggie patties. Ten days of eating for less than two dollars.

George is the building manager/handyman who lives in the basement. He seems easy-going enough, but we're afraid if we ask if we can live in the attic, rent-free and off the books, he'll be forced to say no. We go with the "easier to get forgiveness than permission" adage and move in quietly.

Vagabond Song

After a day of sweeping fifty-year-old dust, laying out bedrolls and building furniture out of milk crates and scrap lumber, we dig in with guitar and typewriter.

> Twenty-six hammers
> Six strings
> Not much to start a revolution
> but we also have hunger & cold
> We have the final light of November
> turning this dancing dust to gold

As we settle in for the night, I worry we'll be evicted as soon as George spots us.

"The thing about a temporary autonomous zone," says Francisco, "is that it's temporary. But coming to an end doesn't imply failure any more than a life coming to an end does."

His words hover in the air and I can tell we're both thinking about the recent deaths of his father and my grandfather and uncle. They all passed within a month of each other, leaving impossibly large holes in our world.

"This may be our only night here," I say, "but even so, it's been a great home."

> First night at Symposia
> wrinkle on the map &
> Chaos holding court
> ghosts of our fathers
> in the blue shadows
> a rooster, a mourning dove
> a flight of wild geese
> feathered dreams fly
> through our separate sleeps

Two weeks later, George bursts through the door to find me sitting at my typewriter in my long johns and stocking cap. He scans our hanging blankets and ramshackle bookshelves and says, "Hey! You got it fixed up real nice in here. You got a car? Can you run down and get me a case a beer and a carton a cigs?"

He hands me a wad of cash, as I'm pulling on a pair of wool pants and slipping into my grandpa's work boots.

"Get yerself one of each, too."

"Um, sure. But we don't smoke."

"Fuck it!" says George – I soon learn this is his motto, drawled out with almost a Down-easter accent, like a displaced lobsterman. "Fuck it! Get yerself two cases a beer then."

We take this as permission to stay.

While holed up in Symposia, we put on a 100th anniversary production of Alfred Jarry's *Ubu Roi* with the lovely madness of Bedlam Theatre. Francisco adapted the script, calling it *One Hundred Years of Pure Shit: A Centennial Aberration of Ubu Roi*. As a playbill/lit zine to accompany the show, I put together the first and last issue of *CaNneD [Chaos Never Died]: A Sympographic Journal of Bedlam*. (We were into long titles in those days, though apparently I still am since the working title for this book is *Dōsojin & Tonic or Thanks for the Ride, Clyde: Neo-Haibun from the Travel-Worn Satchel of a Weather-Exposed Skeleton with the 12-Bars Blues*.)

A1 & THE WICKLOW WAY
seventh movement

RAIN THRASHES THE FEEBLE TENT. The wind rages in gusts and cannon volleys. Every few minutes, a blast of lightning opens up the world and shows our faces to one another, otherwise hidden in the deep black night. A brief camera-flash image of two wandering feralites, *les enfants naturels*, farther away from that mystery called "home" than ever before. We are grizzled and worn from long weeks on the road. We are rain-soaked and bleary-eyed. We are smiling like lunatics.

And I'm thinking, how in the name of Dog did I get here?

It had started simply enough. Yon Acorn showed up one day at the Blue House, where I was renting the attic from a keyboard player friend of mine. A drummer rented the spare bedroom and another drummer lived in the basement. My attic was unfinished, a pile of blankets on the raw floorboards, no heat, a single light bulb and a single window.

It's a sad state of affairs when drummers are given better accommodations than poets, but such was life in those dark days.

Vagabond Song

This was soon after moving back to Saginaw – childhood home of Roethke, who wrote, "We traveled, with hope, and not alone, in the country of ourselves." I had been living in Minnesota at Symposia, another unheated attic where anarchist guitars and experiments in chaos theory kept us from freezing that brutal winter. Francisco and I moved out there after his father and my grandfather and uncle died in quick succession. Three captains in our armada gone, the two of us drifting the Horse Latitudes on a makeshift raft. The Calms of Cancer. Albatross. Sometimes all that's left to do is drive northwest into a blizzard in a van named Earl, to find the attic of an apartment building to squat in, and to ride out the long winter with abandon.

Then, in spring, returning to Saginaw and sharing another attic with Eric Sweetleaf McFish the Cat and a spider who lived on the wall near my head. We had an amicable agreement: he would eat all the silverfish that plagued my attic and I would try not to roll over and squash him in my sleep. The arrangement worked fine, even if he didn't fully live up to his end of the bargain.

Anyway, as I said, Yon Acorn showed up one day and said, "Let's go to Europe."

He had gobs of money from mixing drinks for nouveau riche cardigans on Nantucket. He explained that on Martha's Vineyard the money is old so no one had anything to prove and they tipped for shit. But on Nantucket, the people and their excessive wealth were new acquaintances, so they were all trying to impress each other and tipped extravagantly. Some nights Yon cleared a grand or more.

As for me, I'd squirreled away a couple hundred from working temp jobs – filing dead papers on dead people, moving nondescript boxes from one nondescript room to another nondescript room, sorting identical pieces of plastic because the guy at one auto plant thinks those stamped with a 4 are no good and the guy at the other auto plant thinks the 7s are crap. Not a fortune, but I can get nearly free standby tickets from my brother who fuels jets at O'Hare, and once we got there, our only real expense would come one pint at a time.

We make the arrangements and are in London by the end of the month.

> Landscape of cloud
> below my wing
> hills & plains, cliffs & valleys
> I imagine getting out & going for a walk
> however
> there are 30,000 love letters
> from the jealous earth
> sent to pull me back to her

"What's the purpose of your trip?"

The woman at immigration hates me. She hates my long hair and canvas backpack. She hates my beard and duct-taped boots. She hates that my King George beat her King George. She hates that the Beatles really only became great by leaving her land and coming to mine. She hates that I think you can put a boot in a trunk but you can't put a trunk in a boot.

"What's the purpose of your trip?" she sneers.

Dog-damn, I didn't know I was supposed to have a purpose. These non-nomads have such strange rules.

"Just traveling," I say.

"Tourism?" she accuses, and I think of Paul Theroux, who said, "A tourist doesn't know where he's been and a traveler doesn't know where he's going." But that's not what she wants to

Vagabond Song

hear.

"Okay, sure. Tourism."

"How long do you plan to stay?"

Plan? Jeebus! What is it with these people? Don't they know the wise joke about making Dog laugh?

"About a month or so."

"How much money do you have?"

Ah, now I see what this is all about. The worst crime in a capitalist country is to not have money. You can steal, cheat, maim, murder, start wars, institute genocide, poison rivers, decimate forests, punch holes in the ozone, blow up the moon as long as you're rich. But try to occupy a couple feet of sidewalk and breathe a bit of air without anything in your pocket and you'll be treated like the worst pariah since Cain. He didn't have any money either. If he did, he could have hired a lawyer to get him off free and clear, not to mention suing the estate of Abel for slander, defamation of character and product disparagement.

"About three hundred bucks."

"Three hundred dollars?"

"Yeah, dollars."

Her face disappears into a puckered scowl as if my money were a roadkill skunk. "You can't stay for a month with only three hundred dollars."

"Sure I can. I'll crash with friends or camp out. Hitchhike or walk to where I need to go. My only expense is food, which is cheap if I stay out of restaurants and shop at markets." I decide it's wise to not mention dumpster diving.

Her expression shows no improvement. "You can't work here."

"I don't want to work."

"You can't get a job."
"I don't want a job."
"I'm stamping in your passport that you can't work."
"I don't want to work."
"You can't work."

I'm beginning to see why the colonists were so anxious to get rid of these jerks. She gives me one last elitist glower, stamps my passport like she's squashing a bug and lets me pass.

> We skirt the city, north
> to a small town where a friend
> is generous with tea & space for our sleeping bags
>
> In the morning
> she shows us the trail through Wippendell Wood
> puts an X on the map at Chandler's Cross
> & writes the magic word: "Pub"
>
> Forested from at least 1600
> with public paths that some ancestor of mine walked
> listening to the ancestors of these same birds
> the clacking drum of the spotted woodpecker
> the arresting yaffle of the green
>
> The magic is in the walk
> more than the destination
> though the pints at the end of the trail
> appear & disappear – hocus & pocus

We spend the next few days exploring the brutal walls of Windsor Castle, the whispering crypt of Westminster, the yuppie pubs of London and the farm village of Graveley where my great-great-great-grandfather Charles Peacock married Anne Arbon and then brought the British blood to America. Blood that now flows in me, mingled with that of the Baudin and Desmarais of

Vagabond Song

France and the Martin of Germany. In the shadow of the Graveley church, I search the tombstones for names of ancestors but find none. The town is too small to have a pub, so we head out.

Yon Acorn and I are on the road, hitching north on the A1. We're heading to York, where the grand old duke marched his men up and down the hill, but we don't *know* we're heading to York. We're just heading. North. Out. Into. Beyond. There are only two directions, out and back, and sometimes they trade places without a moment's notice. You may think you're heading back, when suddenly you're getting farther and farther out, and vice versa. It's best not to worry about it and just keep moving. Moving is what it's about. The road knows where it's going.

That's what we're doing on one of those September mornings that try to make people laugh and cry at the same time. We think we might meet the 2,752 from St. Ives but they must have stopped off somewhere to catch 19,208 mice. But at a café for beans on toast (as bad as it sounds), a lorry driver (like a truck driver, but skinnier) tells us he can give us a lift as far as York, if we're going that way. We say we are. We don't tell him that we are only because he has, at this moment, determined that we are. People who think they know where they're going are always confused – sometimes wary, even hostile – when they meet people who know they don't know where they're going. It's usually best to keep it to yourself. Especially if you're trying to hitch a ride.

We make landfall in York a couple hours later and our lorry captain sails off into his own story. Thanks for the ride, Skinny Clyde.

> Roman stones
> still white after so much blood
> the ruins of an empire
> never teach the next emperor
> a goddamn thing

A1 & the Wicklow Way

Circling the city along its ancient walls we shoot imaginary arrows through loopholes down to some invading horde. We scramble through the Shambles, a narrow, crooked street of timber-framed, overhanging, fourteenth-century buildings with doors sized for hobbits. We hide in the shadows of York Minster's mammoth oak doors, listening to the boys' choir singing Latin hymns to *Canis*. We work up a medieval thirst.

A few pints bring us back to the present. Back at our hostel, we lounge on cots in a large communal room scribbling into journals and writing postcards. I write one to a woman I haven't seen in years. The address I have is most likely obsolete and she'll never receive it, but she is the one who comes to me in this history-enchanted city. Maybe it's the light streaming through the windows of the minster or the nostalgia of crumbling stone within the grasp of autumn. Whatever the reason, the image of her on a bench in a hallway at the university, her dark hair hiding her eyes and her patent-leather saddle shoes winking at me from beneath the folds of her long skirt is what comes to me now. We only talked a few times, but somehow, separated by years and an ocean, I find myself thinking of her and what never was nor will be.

The road will do that to a person.

Two days of tourist-town prices and we realize we can't afford to stay in York any longer. We decide to leave first thing in the morning, continuing north. Back in London, our friend had told us about the Holy Island of Lindisfarne – 2¼ by 1½ miles, connected to the mainland by mudflats at low tide, cut off when the tide is in. There is a castle and a monastery, several dozen lobster fishermen and a family that guards the ancient and secret monks' recipe for Lindisfarne mead. Something about the antiquity of Britain, the Celtic whisperings, the unknown burial grounds of my ancestors' bones is making me less a wanderer, more a pilgrim. I'm on my way somewhere, some place with a spiritual presence that I need to let enter me.

We go out for a farewell drink, which turns into drinks and then more drinks. We meet some women who take us to another pub, an underground cavern of loud music and wild dancing shapes jumping in and out of the shadows. We switch from beer to whiskey, which just keeps appearing magically in my hand. A wild dancing shape with dark hair hiding her eyes pulls me onto the dance floor, then into a cab, into her apartment, into her bed. We writhe and roil like it's the end of the world, and for all we know it is. We prove T. S. Eliot wrong, then slip into oblivion.

What would a pilgrimage be without a straying from the path?

In the morning, I climb back to the world of the living with a raging headache and long, deep scratches on my back. I feel like I've been pummeled by thugs and rolled down a rock-strewn hill to a ditch. It's kind of a good feeling.

I navigate the minefield of our detritus scattered across the floor and find a bathroom. When I come back she's awake, leaning against the headboard and looking beautiful in the Sunday morning light.

"Hi."

"Hi."

"Wow."

"Yeah, wow."

"My friend's going to be pissed," I say. "We were supposed to leave early this morning. I can barely walk."

"You're welcome."

We laugh. The exertion hurts. It's time to go.

"So, do you know where the youth hostel is from here?"

"No."

"Okay. How do I get back to the neighborhood where that bar is?"

"Um …" She struggles to the surface. "Go left to the corner, then turn left."

"Okay. Take care."

"Okay." She drifts off as I head into the hall, but then rouses and calls out, "No, wait. Not left. Right."

"At the corner?"

"Yeah. Turn right … I think."

"Left or right?"

"Um, right. Maybe. It's one or the other." And then she's asleep.

I stumble down street after street. Families pass on their way home from church and when they catch sight of this malevolent, stinking cretin from the colonies, they pull their children close and quicken their pace. I fantasize about growling like a beast. Yelling gibberish like "Burn the spiderous legions from the temples of despair!" and "Wainscoting is the devil's hangnail! Long live the Brownian ratchet!"

Eventually I pick out familiar landmarks, cross the River Ouse and lurch through the door of my hostel. I fall into my cot and do my best doornail impersonation.

At some point, I wake to Yon Acorn leaning over me. I begin to apologize for messing up our plans to leave today, but he cuts me off. He's still wasted and the stench of booze oozing from every pore is overwhelming.

"Hey, we can't leave today," he croaks. "I've been up all night with those girls from the bar. I'm going back there to sleep for a while."

"Okay. Goodnight."

When I wake again, there's only one other person in the room – a woman a few cots away who I hadn't noticed before. I listen to the deep breaths of alcohol sleep. Apparently the whole damn town got drunk last night. I get up and struggle down to the showers. The men's shower is being cleaned, but the desk clerk tells me that everyone's gone for the day so go ahead and use the women's.

Once in the stall, with hot water purifying me of all my sins, another person comes in and begins undressing. Must be the woman who was sleeping upstairs. This could get awkward.

"Hello," I venture. "Sorry to invade your shower. They told me at the front desk it was okay."

"No problem," she says, slipping into the stall next to mine. There's only a curtain between us, below our shoulders and above our knees. She smiles and borrows my shampoo. We compare the severity of our hangovers, determine it to be a tie, and decide to go have breakfast together.

Over eggs and tea (dog-damn, I wish this country would discover the vital importance of coffee!) we tell our stories, the legends of how we came to be traveling here. She's from the East Coast, not New York, but close enough to claim it. Her family is in Ireland for a couple years so she split out for a few months on her own. We talk about me visiting her there someday – a big house right on the Atlantic; I could watch the sun drop onto America each night. We both know it won't happen but it feels good to talk as if it might. There's a comfortable romance in our conversation, as if we were old lovers. And then she's gone. Another Vagabond

Angel slipping through the veil that separates my story from hers.

I stay in the café a while, wanting to write a poem, but instead of picking up my pen, I pick up my cup of unsatisfying tea and drain the last of it.

That evening Yon and I find each other, and find a quiet pub. He tells me of his wild night that was much like mine. I tell him I've fallen in love.

"With the woman from the bar?" he asks.

"No, of course not," I say. "With the woman from breakfast."

"So what do you want to do?"

"Hit the road first thing," I say, finishing my pint and letting it hit the table with a satisfying thud.

Pilgrimage to Holy Island

> Forgotten rides
> take us to Newcastle
> feeding horses dried apricots
> across a pasture fence from
> where we've pitched our tent
>
> Awakened near dawn
> by one of them
> pushing its head through
> our unzipped door
> looking for more
>
> My pilgrimage to Lindisfarne
> becomes merely its silhouette
> passing at high tide from
> the grime-streaked window
> of a northbound bus

Edinburgh grabs me right away. Something in the air and the light, the aged black stone spires like dragon teeth – a myth-

Vagabond Song

ical skeleton bricked over but ever present. Our guidebook tells us that the fog that comes in suddenly off the North Sea is the "haar" – a sung word that is impossible to use without feeling like a pirate. We walk High Street and make our way up to the Castle. From there we look out over the Old Town, to Arthur's Seat watching over sea and land, and out to the dark waters rolling over the curve of the Earth. *Keep a weather-eye on the haar, laddie.*

 This city has me. I know my time here will be too short and someday, somehow I will find my way back to the birthplace of Kenneth Grahame, who wrote, "Here today, up and off to somewhere else tomorrow! Travel, change, interest, excitement! The whole world before you, and a horizon that's always changing."

 We slake our thirst on bottomless pints and wake to another day of the murmurings of the old ones. They whisper through each stone and brick. The sea air carries their voices; the eyes of passing strangers carry their memories.

> The light of Edinburgh
> infused by the salt-crisp air
> & breathing, tasting, seeing
> become one song that sings
> through the vibrato-beat
> leaping in my chest

 I could stay here till the money runs out, but Yon has friends in Dublin and I have James Joyce in Dublin, so it's a bus to Glasgow and a ferry across to Northern Ireland. Ever since we arrived in the Isles, Yon has mostly been drinking Guinness, but I've been waiting. I wanted to drink my first *real* Guinness – Joyce's "foaming ebon ale which the noble twin brothers Bungiveagh and Bungardilaun brew ever in their divine alevats, cunning as the sons of deathless Leda" – in Ireland and nowhere else. So I've been drinking instead every sort of bitter, ale and porter, mostly just asking for the local brew. But now I am on the threshold of the best beer in the world. The version of this mad elixir that one gets in the States is an adulterated, sorry ghost of the homeland variety. The night before the boat ride, I dream that as soon as we disembark, I walk straight into a pub and drink a pint of the dark heaven.

The next afternoon, we step onto dry land, exit the shipyard and cross the lane to the pub of my dream. I drain my pint in three deep drafts, wipe my mouth with the back of my hand and loudly quote Joyce: "I was blue moldy for the want of that pint. Declare to God I could hear it hit the pit of my stomach with a click." The regulars, mostly dockworkers and fishermen, pause with hard, confused stares, then go back to their own half-empty pints. No matter. The perfection of the moment is incorruptible.

After another – finished with the same benediction, though more quietly this time – we shoulder our packs and thumb our way south.

We spend the night in a campground that is nothing more than a roadside square of perfectly manicured lawn. It resembles a graveyard, with our tent as the only tombstone – it's getting too late in the year for other campers. The next day, a few rides and one local bus take us to the dorm room of Yon's friends. He worked with them this past summer on Nantucket and they are happy to see him, and instantly welcome me as well.

Our arrival conjures a party with the room filling with college kids loaded for bear with beer and pot. I'm too old for this scene, but as the visiting elder, I pass on some wisdom. The kids are complaining that their pipe is clogged with this "sticky, black gunk" that they have to clean out and throw away.

Vagabond Song

"That's resin," I say.

"What?"

"Give me that pipe." With a penknife, I scrape out the resin and roll it into a BB-sized ball that I drop into the bowl. Handing it back to the confused but about-to-be-enlightened student, I say, "It's a free gift from the pot gods. Smoke it – you'll never complain about black gunk again."

I wake to piles of snoring bodies scattered about the room looking (and smelling) like sea wrack at a harbor after the tide has gone out. Yon wants to lie low for the day, so after a tasteless prepackaged campus breakfast, I hop the bus for downtown Dublin, birthplace, spiritual home, metempsychotic winedark recreation (*life out of life*) of James Joyce, who wrote "babadalgharaghtakamminarronnkonnbronntonnerronntounnthunntrovarrhounawnskawntoohoohooredenenthurnuk!" and "yes I said yes I will Yes."

I walk the streets, looking for the man in the mackintosh. I cross the Liffey in the three hops of McConnell Bridge, wider than it is long, hearing echoes of Bloom and Dedalus. I follow Joyce up and down the trash-blanketed streets and end up at Davy Byrnes, where we drink together and quote each other till we "smiledyawnednodded all in one: –Iiiiiichaaaaaaach!" and become "two fellows who would suck whiskey off a sore leg."

The next time I look up, he's back on the ten-pound note in my pocket and there is a woman at my table. Her name is Gráinne. I stumble over the Celtic pronunciation. She says it means "Grace."

"Amazing," I say.

"... and also Gertrude."

"Like the queen."

"Yeah," she says. "You should write a poem about my name

when you get home and send it to me."

Lost Words for Gráinne

I drop a James Joyce on the bar
pocket the two quid change
& bring the pints back to the table

She holds court with her red hair
& Dublin accent, with words
spilling from a Celtic tongue

A poisoned queen,
a hymn for the lost & found
but then I remember Gertie
& the garter-show at the beach,
the Nighttown vision

She doesn't know the story &
doesn't use that nickname &
I'll probably never write her poem
& if I ever do
she won't remember having asked for it
& I won't have an address to send it to

After a few days of the tug o' war between the suburban inanity of the college dorm and the litter and grime of Dublin, celestial sphere of James Joyce, who wrote, "Every moment of inspiration must be paid for in advance," and "There is an art, Mr Dedalus, in lighting a fire," Yon and I make a plan (insert Dog's laughter – delirious, delighted laughter).

A bus will take us to the village of Eniskerry. We'll load up on pack food and hit out for a three-day hike into the Wicklow Mountains to Glendalough, a seventh-century monastery. I'd never heard of St. Kevin, but a pilgrimage to his house makes as much sense as any other pilgrimage – perhaps more so because

Vagabond Song

I've never heard of him. As Miscellaneous Jones says, "If you're not on a pointless quest, you may as well get a job."

It's a good plan. A great plan. The best-laid plan of ours or any plan-making rodents out there.

Dog is beside himself with glee.

Almost as soon as we leave town, it starts. A sprinkle becomes a drizzle, then a shower, then a rain, squall, downpour, torrent, biblical wrath. Yon and I trudge along the trail, our rain ponchos whipping about us like battle flags. Thunder tumbles across the riven sky as the sun invisibly sinks behind the mountains.

The trail passes a large field edged with trees. We stop and drop our packs.

"Let's make camp here," I say. "This will have to blow over quickly. Tomorrow will be clear and dry."

"Yeah," says Yon. "It has to be."

We struggle with the blasting wind and crowding darkness, but manage to get the tent up and dive inside. We settle in, waiting for the storm to let up, but for hour after hour it only gets worse. We have an old pup tent with two poles held up by guy lines staked in the ground. It keeps the rain at bay but the flashes of lightning pass through unhindered. The wind grows stronger, slashes the air like a hundred grizzlies, their claws rasping the iron sky. Suddenly the fabric of the tent is hitting our faces. I scramble out of my bag and find the door zipper. Outside, I'm instantly drenched. With a fight I get the poles back upright and the stakes back in the ground. A blast of lightning hits, its thunder shadow right on top of it. Way too close. I duck back inside, panting.

"You know those movies where there's a storm at sea and the sailors are fighting with the rigging and waves are crashing over the deck and some are swept overboard?"

"Yeah," says Yon.

"That's exactly what that was like," I say.

This happens three more times. Each time, the wind is stronger, the rain heavier, the lightning brighter. The last time, as I fight the wind for possession of the tent like old what's-his-name wrestling with the angel, a bolt of lightning splinters a nearby tree. The blast is deafening, the flash blinding. I set the stake and dive back inside.

I lie there catching my breath for a few minutes before I'm able to talk.

"Yon?"

"Yeah?"

"We're probably going to die tonight."

"Yeah."

"Beautiful storm, though."

"… yeah."

> Pilgrims bound for an unknown saint
> waiting for death in one instant or the next
> The world is ripped open
> The sky an ocean
> It's been a good journey & the best
> we can hope for is to die
> in the jaws of something beautiful
> & more powerful than ourselves

Somehow the morning comes and we haven't been killed by a lightning bolt or a falling tree. But somehow, also, the storm has not let up. The next scene in movies like this is always a quiet reprieve, with rain dripping from a leaf, a blue sky and then a single bird beginning to sing. Apparently, the Dog of Wicklow in late

Vagabond Song

October is not a fan of such movies.

We stuff our soaking gear into our packs and sludge our way back to the trail. We become dumb, brute beasts, heads down, placing the next step before the last, accepting all the discomforts of the world as nothing more remarkable than our assigned lot in life. Ho-hum. Keep walking.

Blow winds and crack your cheeks – sure, why not?
You cataracts and hurricanes, spout
Till you have drench'd our steeples, drowned the cocks – if you must, what do I care?
You sulphurous and thought-executing fires,
Vaunt-couriers to oak-cleaving thunderbolts,
Singe my white head. And thou, all-shaking thunder,
Smite flat the thick rotundity o' the world – fine. Who am I to suggest otherwise? Do what you will, Sky Dog, I'll just be trudging the Wicklow Way, making ephemeral footprints in the mud.

After an hour or two of this tragicomedy, a smattering of buildings paw their way through the storm to greet us. A sign we half believe to be a mirage reads "Knockree Hostel." As we approach like prodigal bums, a woman darts from a doorway and hens us inside, clucking, "What are you doing out here? You can't be out in this!"

We explain our plan of the three-day hike to Glendalough, attempting to sound reasonable, but she cuts us off.

"No. No. You can't hike in this weather. You'll be killed."

"Well," says Yon, "how about we wait here a bit and let it pass?"

The woman seems saddened by our thickness.

"Oh, dearie, once this weather starts, it's here for at least a month. There's no waiting for it to pass. Come back in summer, but there's no going now."

She gives us use of the community room to dry our gear and clothes while we warm ourselves with oatmeal and tea. Once we've recovered, she arranges a ride back to the village, where we sheep ourselves back on the bus to Dublin, where Yon gets a flight to Paris and I (out of money and nearly everything else) get the ferry to Wales, then the train to London, then the big ol' jet airplane to Detroit, then the 'hound to Saginaw, birthplace of (The One They Call) Al Hellus, brother, comrade-in-ink, fellow *Saginista*, who wrote, "There's moonlight in the woodpulp of this page," and "When the sun goes down the singing will likely commence."

caesura: SQUATEMALA

AN INDEPENDENT NATION of one city block on the fringes of downtown Saginaw. On two of the corners stand immense Victorian houses, three-storied confections of intricate woodwork and stained glass, one topped with a cupola balcony and the other with a copper dome above a tower. "Painted ladies" in their heyday, but now they are faded, decrepit crones with caved-in porches, holes in the roofs, broken railings. In the "Big House" a nest of lovers who share wine and beds, explore a freedom that must, of course, be short-lived. We are sometimes two, sometimes three or four – a delicious decadence that somehow feels innocent and pure. In the "Hill House" a writer in some upstairs room like a ghost, pounding his typewriter by candlelight – a friend's younger brother just beginning a journey on this highway of 26 miles. On the third corner is a one-time carriage house that now holds punk musicians and artists, 40s of Black Label and a haze of pot smoke. The fourth corner has an L of several connected garages, one now a woodshop, another a metal sculptor's studio. A six-foot stockade fence connects the buildings, sealing off the interior of the compound.

Within the fence, the land that was once manicured lawns and gardens has nearly returned to wilderness. Thick with trees and feral plants. Dog-trails, made by Bronx – our Minister of Defense – wind through the dense underbrush past junk cars, stacks of tires and a firepit where we gather nightly, strumming on guitars, drumming on djembes and empty gas tanks, and howling with Bronx at the bloodstained moon.

I was brought in as caretaker. The property owner lives down in Flint and asked if I could live here and keep an eye on things. I didn't think he'd mind if a few friends joined me. A few became a loose community of a dozen or so anarchists and artists, vagabonds and vagrants. We added a three-room tent for visitors, cultivated wild edibles, set up a primitive skills area to teach each other bow-drill fire making, flint knapping, and archery. We declared ourselves a sovereign state and declared war on the money-mind of the U.S.

During one of our bonfire jam sessions, thick with wild dancing shapes in a booze and pot pandemonium, the owner suddenly shows up. I assume I'm about to be homeless. He pulls me aside and looks serious.

"So, having a little party, huh?"

"Uh, yeah," I stammer. "I hope it's okay just this once."

His eyes dance in the firelight as he breaks a smile.

"I think it's great," he says. "I've got a fiddle upstairs, let me grab it and join in."

Our nation grows by one.

We fly through a summer of wild bliss – music and revolution, naked children of the earth. Lovers. Alive. Real.

Squatemala

Fall and winter bring legendary Halloween, Solstice and New Year's Eve parties. A new millennium. On the porch with pots and pans, a trombone, fireworks – gunshots throughout the neighborhood.

In the spring, the U.S. responds to our declaration of war. City workers descend early in the morning with chainsaws, weed-whackers and dump trucks. Our edible plants are branded noxious weeds. Only Chemlawn green carpets are acceptable. The workers assume they are hitting an abandoned property when they knock through our gate and begin cutting. Their concept of the world suffers a serious readjustment when punks, hippies, anarchists and a dog named Bronx flood out from houses, tents and shacks to halt the destruction.

A standoff ensues, centered around the argument over what exactly is a weed. My carrot is his Queen Anne's lace. He knows it's not a carrot – he grew up on a farm. He knows a weed. He knows weeds must be destroyed. I pull out my knife and dig it from the dirt. Bite the wild carrot and offer it to him. As in all of these stupid confrontations, might defeats right and they continue their invasion. Squatemala is conquered. Our people are scattered. Manifest Destiny rears its ugly head once again.

It's just as well. We had our moment. Beauty is ephemeral, which is why it's beautiful. It's time I quit my job, gave up my home, closed out my bank account, cashed in my empties and got back on that gray ribbon of continual wonder. Epiphanies unfolding with each mile.

Westward.

HIGHWAY 2
eighth movement

I wouldn't say I know Highway 2 like the back of my hand. Rather, it's the vein in my wrist. My left. Connecting my writing hand.

The only road I've hitched more is M-52, for years zagging almost weekly between Saginaw and Lansing. Roughly halfway between these points of arrival and departure, in the town of Oakley, there used to be a white garage that faced the road as it ran through town. It was painted with a giant red heart and the words: "Oakley, the little village with the big heart." During one of my trips, I noticed the heart had been covered over with vinyl siding. Here's where Vonnegut would say, "So it goes."

But Highway 2, the vein that flows from the great un-vinyled heart to the dancing pen, is one of the most beautiful routes I've known. It ambles along the northern coast of Lake Michigan in the Upper Peninsula lined on one side with limestone golems breaking from sandy beaches and waving-grass dunes, and on the other with a swaying wall of cedar and spruce. The sky is fretted with the golden fire of gulls, terns, hawks and ravens. Towns with magical names – Epoufette, Naubinway, Nahma Juction – appear from behind easy rises of the flowing road. They offer family-owned diners with fresh-baked pasties, smoked fish and locally collected maple syrup.

On one of countless trips, after a night's camp at Brevoort Lake, an angel lights on a page of my journal for a moment, and is gone before the breakfast dishes are cleared.

Plum

>Late morning sunlight
>pulling the blanket from Lake Michigan
>(asleep & dreaming of ravens)
>climbing the cedared bluff
>& pawing at the windows of a shoebox diner
>
>Her
>at the next booth
>a cascade of hair over bare shoulders
>
>Me
>road weary
>smelling of last night's campfire
>
>Him
>disapproving
>of my beard & ragged clothes
>
>I can't hear the waves questioning the rocks
>I can't remember what I ordered for breakfast
>& I can't see her face
>which is just as well, because
>as she bites into a fresh
>plum
>I can only imagine her lips, nearly the same color,
>her teeth, breaking the fruit's redolent skin

```
          juice gathering at the edges of her mouth
          pausing
          then running to the curve of her chin
          & allowing
               one
                         exquisite
                                             drop
          to fall to her lap
```

To have actually seen such a moment
a man such as I
would have forgotten
why he was on this road
where he was going
& what he would possibly do
once he got there

On the way to Highway 2, I follow up on an invitation to give a reading at a geodesic dome home on Bois Blanc Island. I'm driving Hero, my travel-worn and battle-scarred S-10 pickup. When I first bought him, a decal across the top of the windshield read "CHEVROLET." With the help of a razor blade, it soon read "_HE_RO___." With some black spray paint, the metal emblem on the tailgate became "CHE__OLÉ_." Hero was one of my best ponies, crisscrossing the country numerous times before finding his rest at Rifkin Scrap Metal, the final home of many good ponies. There ought to be a memorial plaque on the chain-link fence:

Here Lies Hero
1991–2006
Good friend for Jesvs sake forbeare
to dig the dvst encloased heare
Blese be y man y spares thes wheels
and cvrst be he y moves my steel

Vagabond Song

I park Hero on a Cheboygan side street, shoulder my pack and walk a few blocks to the ferry dock. The ride to the island reminds me that every journey is a spiritual journey, but a journey by water takes us to the foundation of the soul. In water is our earliest genetic memory, the dreams of our amphibian brain. We are sixty percent water, but it is that sixty percent of ourselves of which we know nothing. It is the mystery we carry, sensed in times of silence or wonder, but never seen. Never defined.

My friend Guillaume meets me at the island's dock with his ever-present pipe jutting from the corner of his whiskered mouth. He's a good old French-radical-war-protester-intellectual with a heart as big as this island where he and his wife make their summer home. The island, as I see during our drive to almost the farthest point from the mainland, is a paradise of ecological history. What has been destroyed and long forgotten on most of the American continent is alive and thriving here. Great stands of maple, aspen, pine and spruce rise from a deep carpet of ferns. The ground is alive with scurrying and chattering flashes of brown and the air is alive with birdsong of every color.

At the dome home, we have beers at the water's edge and watch the biggest garter snakes I've ever seen garland a multi-armed driftwood sculpture. Later, guests arrive with platters of homemade food and we share a potluck. I give my reading, sell a few books, learn and forget names. After everyone leaves and my hosts turn in for the night, I sit staring into the flames of a campfire. The lake is a great silence beyond. The cold bottles give a warm glow to my head and heart. A great horned owl calls out from the darkness and the Milky Way, the Wolf Road, laces the glittering sky. I toast everything with a freshly opened bottle.

Leaving the firelight to better see the stars, I discover clouds of bats darting all around me in a symbiotic dance: I attract mosquitoes with my blood-song to provide their feast, and they free me of the buzz and itch of the purgatorial pests.

Beneath the Wild Rice Moon

> Drunk & dancing with bats
> on Bois Blanc Island
> a bottle in one hand
> a million stars in the other
>
> People in houses behind gates
> in suburbs with meaningless names
> think they are wealthy
> but I am the richest man in the world
> with bats brushing my face & arms
> as I spin myself & the earth spins back

Back to the mainland, back to Hero who has waited patiently but now is ready to run. We cross the Mackinaw Bridge, five impossible miles over the Straits, and pick up Highway 2, westbound.

> Wolf on Highway 2
> dissolves into the forest
> like a bell, unrung

The road mirrors the coastline of one of my favorite bodies of water – the northern end of Lake Michigan, crystalline, memory-cleansing, defying the existence of Gary and Chicago at its other end. I used to take that southern route, when there was a welcoming bed in Grand Rapids and another on a farm south of Kalamazoo. In Chicago, there were friends' couches and my brother's Elvis room, where I slept surrounded by memorabilia

Vagabond Song

of the King: posters, dolls, hair gel, ticket stubs, clothing, cologne, mirrors, photos, autographs, guitars and even Elvis' very own karate black belt. I would go to the Field Museum and stare into the pupil-less eyes of Unis-Ankh, a 4,000-year-old pharaoh's son whose homebound spirit, his *ka*, is in a statue watching over his tomb, now doomed to watch an endless river of gawking tourists. I wanted him to see that I empathized with him. I failed every time.

Chicago

"I want to violently know the world"
says Rilke
as I sit in this Mexican café in Chicago,
mid-journey, waiting for my journey to begin

No one makes eye contact
with a poet in this town
My mind runs around like a feral dog
slave to a thousand scents
but I'm pulled instantly
into monastic focus
when the woman studying chemistry
flips her hair from one bare shoulder
to the other

Later, at the Oakwood
nearing midnight
& the nude on the wall
is as bored as the bartender
who knows but doesn't care
that most amnesia is voluntary
& the moths are full of sorrow
to learn we take the streetlights'
wondrous beauty for granted

But once I discover the northern route, Chicago becomes little more than a historical footnote. This end of Lake Michigan is where new histories are daily created.

There are other bodies of water I love as much as this northern dream-bringer. A small spring-fed lake at Camp Keypayshowink, Lake Atitlán in the Guatemalan highlands, the pool of a spring breathing itself into existence under a fallen spruce in the Absaroka Mountains, the spring runoff along the gutter in front of my grandparents' house when Mosey drained his flooded garden and we raced boats made of bits of litter. I was once told you could see the future in any body of water, and I believe that, though I have no idea how it's done.

Celena

I asked her what she was doing
staring intently at her drink
as the noise of the bar surrounded us like fog

"Watching the future in my glass of vodka," she said
"You can see the future in any body of water
& once you learn how
you'll never watch TV again"

That was the last time I saw her
She used to play the out-of-tune piano
in our backroom
sang beautifully if she thought no one was listening

At her self-scheduled funeral
though I barely knew her
I cried with all the others
when I heard her recorded voice

And every now & then
I stare into a dying river or mug of cheap beer
& try to learn the trick

Vagabond Song

After a fish sandwich and slice of apple pie at a roadside stop, I grab a six to go and find my own isolated beach tucked between sentinels of limestone. I park behind a small dune, strip and run into the welcoming waves. After washing the road grit and nostalgia from my body and watching the miracle of moonrise over black and gold waters, I head back to drink my beer and count my blessings with each star that comes on in the darkening sky, with each wave that breaks on the glistening shoreline. It occurs to me now that the greatest gift I've been given is to appreciate, more and more, the gifts I've been given.

* * *

Years later, I make this journey by thumb, with a full pack. This is after Hero is laid to rest at that eastside scrapyard, and before I buy Clyde, who finds his name on this same road when I realize he and I had traveled many of my old hitchhiking routes: M-46, M-57, M-72 and finally old #2. I pull off the road next to the dam outside of Escanaba, light a sage smudge and christen him, incanting, "Clyde's old diesel rolls to a wary stop and I hop from the cab onto a protest of gravel beneath my duct-taped boots."

The thumb-powered trip starts with some puddle-jumping: K-zoo for a reading where the in-house brew flows free and the night ends in a jam session with new friends. Ann Arbor for a radio gig on WCBN, meeting my host for drinks at the Del Rio, where Coltrane touches the Divine over cranked speakers. Then to Grayling with my spiritual family: bear-hearted Mato, Mari and Shwaa, bonds stronger than blood, born in the waters of Clear Creek in North Camp.

Mato lends me his Jeep to explore the wild swamplands west of Lake Margrethe.

Highway 2

A Good Place

> Across the one-lane bridge
> into the bear swamps
> w/ fiddleheads & the flavor of cedar on the air
> no sound but the hum of the engine
> miles from pavement
> & it seems I'm happiest
> when I find myself
> in one of those places
> about which people say
> This would be a good place
> to dump a body

Next day, Mato takes me to the ramp onto I-75 at the north end of Gaylord. He can't find my trusty old druid's rain poncho that I had lent him when I thought my hiking days were winding down (and that I'm sure was a gift from him in the first place), so we stop at a store and he buys me what's available: a thin yellow thing that rips to shreds the moment I put it on. Standing in the rain unprotected gets me a sympathy ride from two young guys and J.C., a big red dog, who take me over the Mackinaw Bridge and drop me on the dancing ribbon of possibility known as Highway 2.

Stumbling along the graveled shoulder, half-turning to thumb-cast at each passing car, I realize how out of practice I am. My pack feels too heavy – it pulls like some alien object trying to break free rather than hugging like a turtle's shell. My thumb is bent and rusted, falling short of its mark on each cast. The rain is too cold; it's too early in the spring to be up here. A bad mood creeps in like the rainwater through my secondhand boots. I find myself, for the first time ever while hitching, wishing I had a car.

Fuck it. I'm getting too old for this shit. But then, right when

I need them the most, those good old brake lights, the color of angels' wings in the sunset.

The driver has been retired two years and is spending as much time as he has left golfing and fishing his way across the land he never saw from his corner office in Rochester Hills. His happy mutt, Toby, sits on my lap and searches the passing tree line for deer. He takes me into Manistique, where I stash my pack in some dense shrubs and grab a coffee as the rain clears with a cold wind off the lake.

Lighthouse at Manistique

Walking the breaker
into the April fury of Lake Michigan
wind tearing at my clothes
& with each wave shattering
against the limestone
an icy blast across the walkway
holding a momentary rainbow

I have ignored the warning signs
forgotten common sense
am aware of the bone-crashing pain that waits
if I'm swept off & down to the chiseled rocks
& the only reward for the journey –
a few moments in the wind shadow
of the lighthouse, watching gulls
ride the daggers of air

Yet I continue, undaunted
into the blue streaked with sudden rainbows
step after perilous step
& all the time, plastered
to my cold, wet face:
a ridiculous madman's smile

Revived and ready to shoulder that old pack once again, I cast my thumb into the stream of traffic. This time a middle-aged couple hauling a 5th wheel camper picks me up. There's a gun tucked beside his seat, purposefully visible, and an NRA sticker on the window. Not a ride to bring up politics. They're heading to the U.P. state fair to see Jeff Foxworthy make fun of people like them, only poor. The man won't stop talking about guns and Dog and Foxworthy and welfare queens and Jesus and lazy black people and more guns. By the time he drops me off, my tongue is swollen from biting it. Before I jump out, I surreptitiously pull a small card from my bag and tuck it in the pocket behind his seat. It reads:

ADMIT ONE
This ticket entitles the bearer to ENTER HEAVEN
Sin all you want – you're in for free!
Courtesy of the Mist(sic)ical Temple of Moses Om.

It was a gift from Zorba Chaos, but this bastard needs it more than I do.

Then it's a few quick rides – a woman heading to Escanaba to buy aquarium supplies, a man with his five- and six-year-old sons who race pee-wee motocross heading to Menominee to pick up a paycheck for building Coast Guard boats, and some college students heading to Green Bay. They bring me across the border into Wisconsin, birthplace of Antler, who wrote "I should be paid for discovering America is committing suicide with factories!" The students drops me in Oconto. My next ride is a cop.

He tells me hitchhiking is illegal in Wisconsin. That law, plus that it's illegal to buy a motorcycle on a Sunday, rank the state pretty damn high on the list of worst places in the left arm of the

Milky Way. Fortunately, the boggling beauty of its Northwoods redeems it. His lecture continues with the news that unless I get on a bus, the OPD will provide me with a free room and complimentary breakfast. I've had a jailhouse breakfast a time or two. It's an experience better missed.

I try to explain that a bus is a waste of money and that one more ride will get me out of his county – he'll never have to see me again. Unfortunately, he fails to see the logic of my take on the situation.

"When's the next bus leave?" I ask.

"Tomorrow morning," he says.

"So where am I supposed to sleep tonight?" I demand.

"There's a campground back toward town."

I'm getting pissed with his attempts to extort my money for the straight world of buses and campgrounds. Next he'll want me to pay taxes on the air I'm breathing.

"I'm not paying for a campground *and* a bus," I say, probably pushing my luck but too annoyed to care.

He makes a call on his radio and I wonder if I'm going to jail, the hoosegow, the crowbar hotel, the Johnny Cash encore. Instead, he comes back with an offer. There's a city park next to the campground. There's no camping allowed, but he'll make an exception if I promise to get on a bus first thing in the morning.

I'm tempted to point out that he's having me break one law to prevent me from breaking another, but decide to keep that tidbit to myself.

"Okay, but how far back is it?"

"About two miles."

"Christ! I'm not walking back two miles that I just got done walking out."

My attitude somehow works on this guy.

"All right," he says, with an exasperated grin. "Hop in. I'll give you a ride." He even lets me ride up front.

"You know," I say, unable to resist, "it's illegal to pick up hitchhikers in this state."

He laughs, drives me into town, points out a good breakfast place and drops me at the park. I half expect him to give me a hug as I slide out of his patrol car. Dog-damn, this is a strange place.

I find a well-hidden spot in a stand of trees and pitch my tent. I stash my pack a dozen yards away just in case some local spots the tent, then head into town. I figure what I've saved on camping fees should be donated to the neighborhood bar.

Every small-town bar in Wisconsin features either PBR or Old Style. On a drive across once, through towns like Mountain, Langlade, Elton, Athens and Thorp, a friend and I had a contest counting bar signs that featured one or the other. He took Old Style. I had Pabst. I won, 47–44.

Somehow, the bar I find stocks neither. I settle for a High Life and strike up a conversation with the guy on the next barstool. He's another boat builder who breathes fiberglass dust all day because the respirator makes his beard itch. Noah must have had the same problem. My worries that his job is killing him fall on deaf ears. They've been deafened by a desperate need for a paycheck. The American Dream is the biggest serial killer in history – makes Jack the Ripper look like an inept child. I let him buy me a couple bottles with his suicide money, then head back to my illicit tent. In the morning I sneak into the campground and steal a shower. I've decided to break every rule I can in this town. If it were a Sunday, I'd go motorcycle shopping.

Instead, I buy a ticket on the 'hound for Minneapolis. I con-

Vagabond Song

sider just going as far as Green Bay, then going back to hitching, but I'm suddenly tired of it all, feeling old and just wanting to get the hell out of this dog-forsaken state.

By the end of the day, I'm at Francisco's, my comrade/brother/co-conspirator/Didymous from Symposia. We drink Grain Belts and catch up, share new poems, sing temporary autonomous songs and plan the next revolution. With the morning, I walk down to the Seward Café (*Sun comes up, sun goes down*) and order a pot of herbal tea and a Super Red Earth Breakfast, carry my tray to the back courtyard and crack the pages of my journal.

Crossing Time Zones

Sometimes it's a little bird
a sparrow or wren
that holds my life in its beak
Sometimes I am stretched
across the canvas of the sky

I am tormented by the memories
of my muscles

Today, during my fourth cup of tea
a woman with honey skin & flowering eyes
reminds me that I am lonely

This breeze stirs these branches
& what's left of my hair
into the same dance
& for that I am grateful
though it seems now
that every day begins with perfection
& just goes down from there

interlude

Miscellaneous Jones was Redbeard's barber
& farrier to Hannibal
He walked a mile in another man's shoes
then walked a thousand more
He drove the golden spike
for the trans-Utopian railway
stole Columbus' compass
& was the first person
to circumnavigate
the globe of his own watery soul

FLYING CLOUD TO THE WARRIOR TRAIL
ninth movement

CLYDE SOARS ON FLYING CLOUD HIGHWAY, rising and falling with the breathing hills, skirting the two-penny lakes and eye-blink towns of western Minnesota. I'm fresh for travel after a few days holed up in Minneapolis staying at the Shack with Francisco. Guitars and poetry, bucket showers in the backyard, carpentry projects and slinging pizzas at Bedlam. There's talk of another YOU DEAD! show – Franny and me sending our organic words and free-range songs into the air of a coffeehouse, gallery, theater, converted warehouse or other "temporary autonomous zone" as that mad multi-man Hakim Bey would call it. The first one we did was at the Red Eye back in Saginaw. The show was subtitled "Symbiotic Limbo." Other shows in other cities were tagged: "Tell Me the Story of a Soul Wrapped in the Body of a Little Green Toad" and "That's What I Meant. That's Not What I Meant." However, the mania of preparing Bedlam's new theater/community space, this time including a bar and restaurant, squelches the idea for a show. We instead settle for a few songs around the campfire

Vagabond Song

at the Shack, drinking Pig's Eye and eating fire-roasted yams. The poems stay in my head.

I get a late start the next day after filling up on a hearty trucker-style breakfast at the Wienery, where the bacon is thick, the mugs are chipped and the eggs are cooked to perfection. I fill my travel mug with strong, gritty coffee from the Hard Times Café and hit the road.

But Dog-Dog-Dog! Sometimes the present moment jumps in and says, "Hey! Listen! Now!"

>At the helm of this
>mid-morning-sky blue
>Royal Mariner with hammers clacking
>Hamid Drake plays his tabla &
>Fred Anderson plays his soul
>All my fathers and brothers
>watch over me from my writing wall
>& I don't mind at all
>that my coffee's gone cold

Nearing dusk I hit the South Dakota state line. I haven't seen another car in miles. If you've never been out on the prairie, far from the lifeless slashes of the interstates, it's hard to imagine the quality of silence here. In the Midwest or on either coast, there are silences, but they are small silences. Contained. Limited. ... Out here, with endless, gently undulating waves of grass stretching to a 360 horizon, with a sky simultaneously boundless and close enough to touch, the silence is pervasive. Elsewhere, silence is the lack of something. Out here, it is the presence of something. Something unshakable.

Driving 212

Out here on these South Dakota two-lanes
where the prairie chickens outnumber
the cars ten to one

& you can squint the endless
bales of hay
into ghost-herds of bison

where the horizon is a full circle
enclosing you like a
cello sonata in E minor

if you stop your truck &
take a few steps
into the sagebrush & needlegrass

you'll be swallowed by a silence
that exists nowhere else
in the world

If you stand there long enough
with the sun teaching
your shadow to dance

the grains of sand will replace
each cell of your body
one note at a time

& you will begin to understand
something
about this land

Sometime after dark, I pull into a campground on Whitlock Lake, where the Little Cheyenne flows into the Missouri. There's no registration booth, just a pipe to drop your money in. When I drive back to the sites, I see I'm the only one here. An entire campground to myself – not the first time this has happened in South Dakota. A short walk in the turquoise moonlight, a few minutes scratching the pages of this journal and a welcome sleep. In the morning I strip and splash the frigid lake water over my body and greet the day.

I soon cross the Missouri River, over a rustic and finely sculpted trestle bridge, into Mountain Time. With the crossing, I enter the Cheyenne River Reservation, in bad need of some coffee. Flying Cloud Highway becomes the Warrior Trail.

Whenever I'm traveling these sprawling rez lands of the West, through these harsh and abstract spaces, I feel like I've entered an altered reality – something mythical and mystical is at work here. I don't say this for any of that New Age glorification of Indigenous cultures mumbo-jumbo, which is usually little more than racist appropriation for profit among the leaders of the New Age movement and soft-headed, dime-store therapy among the followers. Everywhere is Indian land and all land is sacred – a box drawn on a map by a thieving *wasicu* doesn't create a magical zone. The government's illegal decision to limit the Native peoples to open-air concentration camps doesn't engender sacred space; yet, paradoxically, unintentionally, unwittingly, it does.

Because of the offensive existence and immoral management of the Bureau of Indian Affairs, because of the third world living conditions and lack of access to resources, because these lands were chosen by their uselessness to the ruling class (useless, that is, until gold, silver, uranium, oil, coal or any other crack rock of capitalism is discovered there – then it's time to "negotiate" new borders), because of all of this, these lands remain mostly undeveloped, untouched by "modernization." A loaded word that is mostly a euphemism for commodification and destruction of the

Flying Cloud to Warrior Trail

natural. Inadvertently, the government has set up small islands that are preserving the ancient power of the American landscape. Living museums of what the Europeans encountered and either fell in love with or, out of the misguided fervor of their corrupt, earth-hating religion, sought to destroy. Either way, they were forever changed by it.

The same is true for other lands that have been spared or resisted development: wilderness areas, parts of some national parks and wildlife refuges, the too-harsh-for-condos lands of the desert south and frozen north, and feral urbanscapes like Squatemala (R.I.P.). You can visit these spaces and feel this same energy, hear the voice of the land speaking through your bones. However, these non-casino reservations of the West add another component: community. You can find towns and villages where people are living in such a way that the land, despite the televisions and cars, still has a primary impact on their collective psyche. You can feel the difference when you talk to the people out here; you can see it in their eyes and hear it in their laughter. We came close at Squatemala, but our attempt at autonomy was short-lived, doomed from the start. But the feeling I get out here is the same that I felt with the Mayan peoples of southern Mexico and Central America – never in the general population of the urban U.S. It's the combination of community and a connection to the land that creates it. The first by itself breeds insularity. The second without the first breeds isolation. For the bulk of my life, I have known one or the other, rarely both together.

The tragedy here is, of course, the implication that poverty and its attendant sufferings are somehow necessary to create these conditions. I pray to Dog it's not true, and I don't believe it is. The pre-capitalist Lakota had less money and were far richer,

Vagabond Song

and the post-capitalist People will be rich again. I have no idea how this transformation will be made possible, but I do know that Lucy Parsons was right when she said, "Never be deceived that the rich will allow you to vote away their wealth."

It will take more than that. Democracy is in the streets.

I'm mulling over these thoughts while having breakfast (and that much-needed cup of coffee) at a small diner in Eagle Butte. The woman behind the counter is wearing a T-shirt with a picture of four Apache warriors and the words "Homeland Security: Fighting Terrorism since 1492." There's a white cop chatting with her over the coffeepot, either oblivious to her message or used to it. Or maybe in agreement with it and only has the job he does to feed his children and pay his mortgage.

I fill up my travel mug and go back out to Clyde. There are flies all over his windshield, feeding on the dead bugs I've slammed into the past couple of days. A feast of the dead. A corpse buffet. Probably a bad sign. Better keep driving.

Miles of dust and sun. The land speaks into my bones. Hours spin away like dust devils. I drive on, squinting through Clyde's bug-covered windshield. From time to time, I pull off the road and wander the open land. My palms brush across the heads of bluestem and Junegrass. Unseen curlews call with their ocean voices and meadowlarks flash their sun-painted throats from fenceposts. The rasping of grasshoppers gives way to the chirping of field crickets as the day surrenders to another night.

The Drive

Dakota moon
on prairie potholes
dappled with silhouettes
of long-necked birds

Flying Cloud to Warrior Trail

Radio turned off &
windows rolled down
to breath in this night
this defiant dance of grass

The distant shimmer
of heat lightning &
my windshield a massacre
of insects

The grasses remember
every passing
whether hoof, wheel
fire or plow

My machine & I
grind on
The death toll rising
with each mile

The grasses remember

* * *

THE FIRST TIME I CAME THROUGH THESE LANDS was with Hero, the S-10 with a heart of fire. I took a more southern route to go to Pine Ridge and the Badlands. That journey really began when I stated my intention for an *Inipi* ceremony. That was the moment of departure. It was a journey that lasted ten years, maybe more.

> *Waabanong daasi manido.*
> *Zhawanong daasi manido.*
> *Au-pung Gizhimook daasi manido.*
> *Kiiwedinong daasi manido.*
> *Ishpaming daasi manido.*
> *Aki daasi manido.*
> *Nawaii daasi manido.*

The pipe is offered to the Seven Directions. A circle of cedar laid-out in these borrowed woods. Our lodge built at the western doorway, facing east. I've participated in Anishinaabe sweats before, but our Water Pourer has received training in both Anishinaabe and Lakota traditions, so our lodge is a coming together of both. We've spent the last four days preparing tobacco bundles, abstaining from drink and negative intentions. We smudge with sage and enter the womb of the Earth. *Mitakuye Oyasin.* For all my relations.

I was born into a culture defined by its lack of culture. A middle-of-the-block house in a midsized mid-Michigan Midwestern town. Dragged to a Methodist church where the singing was flat and muttered, and the slightest show of religious fervor made everyone uncomfortable. Communion felt as spiritual as the coffee and cookies after the service. For the rest of my week, school was little more than a daily taste of prison. Forced to line up, boys on one side, girls on the other, before coming in or going out. Forced to stand and recite the propaganda of allegiance to a vicious lie. Forced to read books by dead white men that celebrated the deeds of other dead white men. Daily fistfights on the playground, sometimes in the halls or overcrowded classrooms.

By an early age, I felt that the left hand of the church and the right hand of the state were playing three-card monte with my mind, body and soul and there was no way to win. There never was a queen to flip over. I felt no connection to any of it. If this was my so-called culture, I wanted no part of it.

The one place I did feel I belonged was the forest. Among the trees, I found my church and school. I found something worthy of allegiance. My culturalization began in my grandparents' apple trees and the overgrown alley behind our house. Later it was at the summer camp where I spent four summers as a camper and seven summers on staff as the nature director. As soon as my classes were done for the day, I would head out into "North Camp," across the lake from the program areas and campsites. I'd spend hours out there, sometimes with Mato, a close friend and brother – a closeness forged by this place. But more often I was alone, just walking, sitting, watching, listening. I was gaining a deep connection with the plants and animals, with stones and the lake. I was developing what I came to refer to as "EarthHeart" – a fully immersed and unified relationship with the natural. I found that there were myriad presences out there that could be known and communicated with. They became my teachers and guides, mentors and ministers. They taught me a religion built on direct experience and physical realities. I came to know that any religion that comes from a book is false – one must go to the source to know truth.

This connection with the Earth led to a connection with cultures outside of my own that also had such a connection. Since I lived in the land of the Great Lakes, where the rivers were the first highways and the later highways were built on ancient trails that led from maple-sugaring camps to wild-ricing camps, the cultures of the Ojibwa and Odawa resonated most strongly. I was invited to join a powwow drum group of mostly white guys who had also come to a connection with this culture beyond the one they were born into. At powwows, a common T-shirt for sale simply had the identifying word "Anishinaabe." We joked that we should make shirts for ourselves that said "Anishiwannabe." But it *was* just a joke. We weren't trying to pretend we were something other than what we were. For myself, this was the only living culture of my homeland that reflected the belief system taught to me by the forest. An organic flowering of my path led to a tradition that had been traveling that same path for millennia. A Native friend once told me that whites should stick to their religion, meaning Christianity. But that's not the tradition of my people any more than living in tarpaper B.I.A. shacks and trailers is his. Christianity is a religion of invasion and forced submission. My people were practicing an Earth religion before the "Holy" Roman Empire forced the cross on them with swords and catapults.

An Odawa friend invited me to my first sweat lodge, *Madoodiswan* in Anishinaabemowin and *Inipi* in the Lakota language – "Come back to life." It changed me in a way that can't fit into any house of words. Song could hold it, or dance, but not these twenty-six tricksters of ink.

Since then, it's how I mark the most significant moments of my life.

Before setting out on the road trip that would take me into the heart of the sacred, I needed to prepare with this ceremony. I planned on visiting the site of the Wounded Knee massacre of 1890, and *Paha Sapa*, the Black Hills. I needed to prepare and I needed to ask permission. Both could be done in the purifying steam of the lodge.

> The Stone People talk
> red tongues cleaving the darkness
> Spirit Roads open

After the ceremony, we crawled like newborn babies from the dome of willows and saw what we took to be lightning filling the sky to the east. Then we realized it was the Fourth of July and back in the city everyone was celebrating a very different form of independence – out here, our independence was synonymous with interdependence. The light show was inside; fireworks paled in comparison. I took the long way home, avoiding the frenzy.

* * *

I-75 TO THE BRIDGE, Highway 2 to the border, 64 to the Twin Cities for a reenactment of Symposia, our mad and magical attic of whim and wonder, Discordia ruled and Chaos never died, where Miscellaneous Jones laughed across the chasm between that world and this.

Not all who ponder are sauced. But it helps.

Out of the city – away from the grid, I head south on 35 and pick up 90 West ... west, that direction of directions, the question mark on the compass, that place on the map where the ink fades to nothingness. *Hic svnt Dracones.*

I'm trying to decide whether to stay on the expressway or take back roads. If I choose back roads, I'll cut up Highway 75, called the "King of Trails," to Pipestone and take 34 into South Dakota. Which I choose, of course, will make all the difference in the world. As William Least Heat-Moon says, "Life doesn't happen along interstates. It's against the law." Those routes have been anesthetized for your protection. Movement is an illusion: the billboard cowboy wears the same hat in Abilene as Atlanta. The genetically bastardized McDestruction-of-Local-Flavor-and-Sucker-of-Souls-Burger tastes the same in Sacramento or Syracuse.

Just as I'm thinking I should go to the Pipestone Quarry, that maybe I'll gain something there to help me at Wounded Knee, a great blue heron flies over me heading in that direction. Of all the messengers that visit me from time to time, Heron is the strongest. If I have a totem, this is it.

Another Blue (*Ardea Herodias*)

Voice of the heron carries the
rasp of pterodactyl & archaeopteryx
Is an unmarked grave that reaches

suddenly with taloned fingers &
startles the man swimming alone
among cattails & mud-sleeping turtles

He once, years before, carried a dead heron
to his chest like an infant – this old
friend & father, teacher in the school of

lake water & moonlight, omen,
bringer of dreams, found in the reeds
at lake's edge, waiting

From his canoe, aluminum turned brass in
evening light, he watches the bird's spirit, or
something, fly from the willows, bank above

the still water & disappear over the mosaic
of trees climbing the hillside. Today
standing thigh-deep in the marsh

he rubs that memory between thumb
& finger, enjoys the sun sinking into face
& shoulders & tries to ignore

the insistent buzzing of an airplane
like some small insect, trapped
at the kitchen window

    The Pipestone Monument holds the traditional quarry for catlinite, the stone used for ceremonial pipes. It's where the stone for my pipe came from. At Little Elk's Retreat back in Michigan, a friend spun around in front of me during a Crow Hop dance and placed the pipe in my hand, then danced off into the circle before I could thank him.

I hike a mile loop through the quarries and past Lake Hiawatha. Goldfinches, robins and a catbird accompany me. At the "Oracle," a natural rock formation of a woman's face that juts from a cliff, I feel the presence of the other side. But it's just a vague sensation. If there's a message here, I don't know what it is. I raise, then lower my camera. A photo would be an insult.

Back at the visitor center, I smear some Pipestone dust on my medicine bag and head back out to my truck.

On the road, I rise and fall on slight waves through grasslands pierced with prairie potholes. These small ponds are the continent's incubator of waterbirds. At each one, I scan for herons, often seeing one stalking fish among the ducks and geese. The road is at times blanketed with killdeer, mourning doves and, new to my life list, yellow-headed blackbirds. I pass a handful of domestic bison in a field and try to imagine the multitudes they once were, herds stretching upwards of fifty miles, until their slaughter became official policy in order to starve the Indians onto reservations. If I squint my eyes just right, the endless bales of hay look like buffalo lounging in the grasses.

That night, I find a campground on a bend in the Missouri River that separates the Crow Creek Rez from the Lower Brule. The camp is on the Crow Creek side. It isn't what I would call a campground. Rather, it's a grass parking lot for RVs with generators attacking the night. My tent is a shantytown to their humming high-rises. I heat water on my zip stove and throw in a handful of orzo and a veggie bouillon cube and give it a stir. With a slab of cheese and a good drink of water, it's a feast for kings.

The next night, I camp in the Badlands with a moon bright enough to read by. Clouds peel from its surface like corn husks. A continually shifting show of lightning over Pine Ridge to the south. Wind gusting at times till it seems it will shred my tent.

It's supposed to reach 100 degrees tomorrow. Should make for some interesting hiking. I'll try for an early start and retreat to a rare patch of shade for the afternoon.

Domestic Feral (*Columba Livia*)

Her trident feet know the pavement like
I know these four walls. We both
feed at the mercy of others, pace

like prisoners or pendulums, see
our reflections in glass buildings &
dream of cliffs. There was a time

when she was not a pigeon & I
was not a citizen, a sapiens, a wearer
of shoes & hats, & then

in the searing silence of the Badlands
I see them darting in & out of shadows
primordial, pre- & post-historic:

Rock Doves
in & of themselves, free &
fearless & I for a moment

can imagine myself barefoot
to the earth, bareheaded to the sky
unthinking fearless & free

Flying Cloud to Warrior Trail

Hiking the Medicine Root trail with the sun taking its toll after a couple of hours in the near 100-degree heat. I make for a rare cottonwood sprawled over a coffin-width muddy trickle. I want nothing more than to lie in whatever water is there and cool off, maybe nap through the rest of the afternoon. When I get to the tree, I find a protecting circle of dense poison ivy. The water is off-limits, but at least I can get close enough to the tree to enjoy some shade. I watch a dragonfly lazing among the leaves, listen to the meadowlarks invisibly calling from somewhere to the north, and take long, hot drinks from my canteen.

Back in the annihilating heat, I scan the arid landscape that was once the floor of a sea. Eroded cathedrals of banded rock – rust and ochre, sienna and ebony – stand silent in the rage of the sun. Suddenly, I can see it, or rather feel it: the vastness of water, the strange prehistoric fish hovering in the depths. The salt scent of this ancient sea mingles with today's aromas of sage and flaking limestone – or is it merely the salt of my own sweat that conjures this image?

The distinct sound of hoof beats approaches from behind. When I turn, there's nothing there. I move to continue walking and hear it again. In my imagination, I see the horse and rider. A large tobiano pinto stepping deliberately across the rock. A Lakota man in traditional dress. I can hear the jangling of claw and bead ornaments, the rain-whisper of dewclaw-covered arm and leg bands, but no creak of a leather saddle. He rides bareback. The image is clear and the sound is real. When I turn, nothing. No one.

This happens four times.

> Time melts & blurs
> under this brutal sun

> vision leads by following until
> I stand before a stone medicine wheel
> placed on the crumbling floor of rock
>
> A photo of it now sits on my writing desk
> a drawing, in the wingtip of the crow
> tattooed on my back
> yet all these years later
> I still struggle to quite believe
> in the truth of such a truth

A late-afternoon storm blasts across the land as I park Hero and climb to a high spot overlooking Bigfoot's Pass. This is where Chief Spotted Elk, nicknamed Bigfoot, and his band of Ghost Dancers came through the wall of rock on their way to an appointment with the Ghost Shirt–penetrating bullets of the 7th Calvary at Wounded Knee. I try to break through the veil of time again and call down to them to turn back. To warn them of the coming slaughter, the frozen corpses, the mass grave.

The sky tears open like innocents before a Hotchkiss gun and the rain pounds me. Thunder and lightning exchange quick blows, and it occurs to me that I am the highest point for miles around. A flesh and bone lightning rod. I meekly creep back to Hero and head for lower ground.

By the time I make it back to my camp, the storm has murdered my tent. It clings to the earth by one remaining stake. Its seams have been clawed apart by the deft fingers of the wind. After the storm passes, I tie a tarp across the bed of the pickup, using a section of salvaged tent pole to raise the center, and crawl inside. With the rubber bed-liner and tailgate open for air flow, this proves to be a more comfortable home than the tent was. Creation always comes from destruction, even for something so mundane as a place to sleep.

In the morning I head into Pine Ridge, passing through the town of Scenic. Both "town" and "scenic" are open for debate. I gas up across the road from a bar sagging under the weight of hundreds of cow skulls and a sign that says "Indians Allowed." The painted-over "No" at the beginning of the message is still visible. The next sign I see as I drop south is much better:

ENTERING
PINE RIDGE
INDIAN RESERVATION
LAND OF THE OGLALA SIOUX
CHIEFS
RED CLOUD   BLACK ELK   CRAZY HORSE

Wounded Knee. Ask for healing. Offer tobacco for those murdered, those living. Take a handful of dust and throw it, imitating Yellow Bird's defiance. It blows to the west. A golden dragonfly accepts the offering. As I drive away, I'm nearly in tears.

I recover with lunch at the Cuny Table Café, where Millie fixes me the perfect grilled cheese sandwich, just like my grandma used to make. I wash it down with a tall iced tea and order another of each. Millie is also the person to ask permission for access to the Stronghold Table, considered to be the most sacred area of the Badlands and the spot where the Ghost Dance was last performed before the massacre. Of course, since the U.S. seems determined to reach the lowest circle of Hell, this is the land they stole during World War II to use as a bombing range. After blasting it into ruin and leaving it littered with shrapnel and unexploded, highly dangerous ordnance, they gave part of it back, deciding to keep a piece for themselves to entertain history-buff tourists.

Millie describes the gates to pass through, the two-track through the grass to follow. I drive slowly to keep the dust down, but also because this is how one should approach places like this.

Suddenly the trail disappears, along with the entire prairie around it. The world drops away into a maze of stone. I park and begin the descent.

I wander in silence, place tobacco and dance a slow circle. A souvenir of paradox: I find a .50 caliber bullet that *wasn't* used to kill some child soldier on the *other* Western Front.

Over near Red Shirt, on one of these trips out here that mingle and merge in my memory, I meet up with the Red Feather Development Group to help build a straw-bale house for the Fast Wolf family. We work long, hard, happy days. Nights, I keep mostly to myself.

Southeast of Red Shirt

>Walking at night
>down the pale scar
>of an unpaved two-track
>in this remote corner
>of the Pine Ridge Reservation
>
>A blanket of stars
>is pulled overhead
>& the unforgiving prairie
>stretches
>to a vast circular horizon
>
>Coyote's song rings in my ear
>like the afterglow
>of a lightning flash
>To the east
>the ancient skeleton of the Badlands
>dances
>unseen & silent

Then I hear
three gunshots to the north
& the temperature drops
a good ten degrees
& now that I know
I am not alone in this world
suddenly
I am alone

As the house nears completion, we take an afternoon off for a swim. I have the honor of meeting what becomes another of my favorite bodies of water.

River Music

Floating, eyes closed
face to an unclouded sky
held by the cool hands
of the Cheyenne River
I forget – for a moment –
the uranium from inhuman mines
seeping
into each pore of my body
like late-afternoon sunlight into every window in town

The uranium I myself put here
by paying my taxes
by shopping for a bargain
by reading the lies of American history textbooks
by watching the propaganda of John Wayne
    on Sunday afternoons wrapped
    in a blanket the colors of the flag
by thinking that wisdom is to be found
in the books of dead men
    rather than in the song of the nighthawk
    or the poem of cottonwoods clacking in the breeze

I float, apart from myself

allowing the river to carry me like a vapor
my feet dragging through muck and over rocks
weeds & small fish
brushing my legs in velvet greeting

The sun through pale eyelids
becomes a field of sunflower
the voices of the Native children
downstream –
bees darting
among the golden heads nodding in the wind

They transform this poison nectar into song

And in my broken Lakota
with my funny city-bred accent
I try to sing along:

> *Wanbli gleshka waniyan nihiyouwe*
> A spotted eagle is coming for you

When I stand & stagger to the shore
dry off & climb into my truck
I hope the toxins I have absorbed
will leave this river
some small part cleaner

& will shine on my skin like a mirror

Paha Sapa – the Black Hills. A pine and rock paradise in the midst of prairie bleakness. All the streams run fast. I break park rules and collect sage. But I offer tobacco and ask permission first. There are greater laws than those of men.

At one point, my map shows two roads, one of which goes past Mt. Rushmore – the most heinous desecration of a sacred space to ever occur. Those four conquerors staring down at their stolen land. As presidents go, these four are far better than most.

They all worked toward some admirable goals and accomplished much that could serve as a fine lesson to us all. When it comes to their Indian policy, however, they deserve our contempt. And in the case of a monument to them carved into the most sacred place of the Plains tribes – a place stolen in direct violation of constitutionally binding treaty – their Indian policy *is* the central issue, the record by which we must judge them here.

There's George who, in regard to the Seneca, ordered his general to "lay waste all the settlements around … that the country not only be overrun but destroyed" and to not "listen to any overture of peace before the total ruin of their settlements is effected." There's Thomas, who called for all Indians to be "exterminated or driven beyond the Mississippi" and that it was preferable to "extirpate them from the earth." There's Teddy who said, "that the [Indians] recede or are conquered … is due solely to the power of the mighty civilized races who have not lost their fighting instinct, and by their expansion are gradually bringing peace into the red wastes where the barbarian peoples of the world hold sway." And there's Honest Abe, who ordered the largest mass hanging in U.S. history. It was punishment for an uprising caused by his refusal to pay a legally bound debt to the Santee. He then forced the removal of every Dakota Indian from Minnesota.

Two roads. One goes to Rushmore. I take the other.

* * *

YEARS LATER, and I'm finishing my breakfast at that diner in Eagle Butte, up there on 212 – "Flying Cloud" in Minnesota, but out here it becomes the "Warrior Trail." Miles of dust and sun. The land speaks into my bones. I drive on, squinting through Clyde's bug-covered windshield.

I've been considering this for the past few years, but now I'm sure: I must go to Bear Butte, *Mato Paha*, one of the most sacred places on earth. The place where great people like Crazy Horse and Black Elk went for vision and guidance. One of my elders (a concept severely lacking in white culture) told me years ago that I needed to go there. Each time I passed through this area, there were excuses masquerading as reasons to put it off. But now, all feels right, no excuses ambush me and I have the right supplies (smudge stick, tobacco, pipe). Today I will make my steps on *makoce wakan*, sacred land.

After leaving Eagle Butte, I drive for about an hour and stop at the Ben Ash Monument, which marks the spot where Ash and a few other white trespassers first spotted the Black Hills. I walk several yards to the southwest and scan the horizon. Nothing. Perhaps they had better eyesight or a clearer day. Or maybe this was just a more convenient spot to stick the marker.

Several miles down the road and I have my own Ben Ash Monument: From the blue-gray ashen haze of the horizon, suddenly pulling away in silhouette, I see a darker shape. The Black Hills, Paha Sapa, also makoce wakan. For the Lakota, the center of the universe. And then, to the left, rising far higher than I expected, Bear Butte. A mountain island floating in the middle of the sea of grass. I can't take my eyes off it. Something grabs hold of my chest and I can feel my heart beating in my throat. The sensation grows stronger the closer I get. Then I'm there.

Using Clyde as a windbreak, I light sage and wash the purifying smoke over my body. Cleansed, I'm ready to enter into the Sacred. I pack my pipe, water bottle and journal into a small daypack (all also smudged) and begin to make my way up the trail.

Flying Cloud to Warrior Trail

Almost immediately, my calves and knees are aching. I'm in the worst shape I've ever been in and living in mid-Michigan doesn't provide much opportunity to train for a climb. But after ten minutes or so, the pain melts away and I feel great – alive and energized and free of the weaknesses of this old body of mine.

Everywhere I look, prayer ties speckle the trees marking hundreds of people, year after year, who have come here to pray. As I climb, the trees become more stunted, the trail steeper and rockier, my thoughts quieter. I am wrapped within the vast silence of the prairie.

Finally, the last few steps and I'm at the summit. But something is wrong. I am not standing on the top of this sacred mountain. I am instead on a wooden observation platform raised a foot above it. There is a railing corralling me into a small square and I think: those bastards have done it again. Every sacred space in America gets desecrated and belittled through ignorance.

I'm reminded of a journey, years ago, into the womb of the Earth at Carlsbad Caverns in New Mexico. After a two-hour descent into darkness and solitude, I came to the deepest cavern, the very heart of the vision walk, only to find a gift shop and snack bar and even a dog-damned elevator shooting people down from the surface so they could snap a few pictures, eat a hot dog and buy a T-shirt.

Granted, this isn't quite as bad as that, but I came here to make my steps on Mato Paha, not a manmade platform.

And then I notice something beautiful: off to the north, the spine of the mountain runs for another forty yards to a cluster of shrub-like trees filled with prayer ties – and this spot is several feet higher than where I now stand. My apologies to the South Dakota Park Service: They didn't destroy the summit, they saved

Vagabond Song

it. By building this platform, they keep the ninety-nine percent of people who are here as tourists *off* the summit. Perfect. I slip over the railing and respectfully make my way to the true summit.

I offer tobacco to the Seven Directions and sit on the rock. I slide my pipe from its bag and assemble it: the sumac stem made for me by the friend who invited me to my first Madoodiswan ceremony, and the catlinite bowl given to me by the friend who invited me to my first powwow. I fill the bowl with *asema* and offer the pipe to the Seven Directions. But when I try to light it, the steady wind makes it impossible. No matter how I cup my hands, how low I crouch, there's just no way I'll ever get it lit. I wonder if I should head to lower ground with more cover to pray. I worry that I'm being told I shouldn't try. But just as I'm about to give up, a passing vulture breaks from his path and flies directly toward me. He's at eye level and only a few yards away when he banks up and hovers, seemingly motionless. At that exact moment, the wind stops. I light my pipe. The great bird veers off and the wind comes blasting back. I make my prayer.

> Mitakuye Oyasin
> Black-feathered one takes the wind
> Smoke calls out to sky

After Bear Butte I head northwest, clip a corner of Wyoming and eventually hit Montana. A few miles after getting back on 212, I pass a hitchhiker. I'm not sure why, but I don't stop. This is totally out of character for me. Clyde (my truck's namesake) has his "Five Rules to Live By," one of which is "Always pick up hitchhikers." I follow this and the other rules whenever I can.

With his characteristic mirth, Clyde had told me his five rules: "Number One is always talk to strangers. If you don't you'll

Flying Cloud to Warrior Trail

never have any friends. Number Two is always pick up hitchhikers. Lucky for you. Number Three is always give anyone anything they ask for. Everything I have is a gift, so is meant to be passed on. And Number Four is always allow anyone to do you a favor. If you deny someone else the chance to be generous, you're preventing them from improving their soul, and you're keeping the world one more step away from Heaven."

"What about rule Number Five?" I asked.

"Number Five," he laughed, "is always be on the lookout for Rule Number Five."

It seems like a pretty good code of ethics to me. Ever since, I've done my best to live by them. Especially after the countless rides and acts of kindness strangers and angels have given me, I usually go out of my way to get hitchhikers to where they're going. But this time, I just drive by.

I feel guilty right away – begin to worry about the karmic repercussions, but still I don't turn back.

Maybe I don't want the spell Bear Butte has cast to be broken. But more likely, it's that too much time of not being on the road, breathing the concrete and smog, suspicion and isolation of the city, has made me cold. Whatever it is, I drive on into the thickening dread of my bad karma.

Just after the Montana border, I enter the town of Alzada on the Little Missouri River. Their one gas station is trying to gouge people for $3.39 a gallon. Every place I've seen on this trip, no matter how small or remote, had prices hovering around $3, mostly below. I have a little under a quarter tank left and my map shows two other towns on the way that are near enough, so I mentally flip them off and drive on.

When I find that the next two towns have no gas stations, and

I'm now well under one-eighth of a tank, I sense just how Old Man Karma is going to kick my ass.

As the miles unroll through the harsh barrenness, I slow down and roll up the windows in a nearly useless effort to conserve gas. When the next town turns out to be nothing but a crossroads with a long-closed store and a couple of barns, I know I'm in trouble. As my needle dips below E, I start wondering if one of the very sporadic ranches I pass would have any gas I could buy, but I realize if they did, it would only be diesel.

I'm looking at a long, very hot walk on an empty road to find gas and a long, very hot walk back. This also means finding a place to crash for the night as it will then be too late to make it to my cousin Doug's place outside of Livingston. Finally, with the engine sputtering in near defeat, I begin a thankful descent into the town of Broadus and coast on fumes into a gas station. And even though I'd gladly pay anything, they're only charging $3.13. I fill up my tank and begin to breathe again.

The next hitchhiker I see is going to get a ride right to his front door. I'll even carry him across the threshold and tuck him into bed.

With the stress of an empty tank gone, the drive is beautiful again, rising through the Northern Cheyenne and the Crow Reservations, the latter home of the Little Bighorn.

The last time I came this way, I stopped so I could dance on the spot where Custer died for his sins, but there was an entrance fee so I turned back. A few years later, I would go to the monument, but it was all just too tragic and stupid and pathetic to dance. I stared at the markers for a while then left with nothing to say.

Eventually I drop onto the interstate at Billings. In a quick two hours, I'm entering Livingston, home of Michael Earl Craig, who wrote, "It's a poet's job to be dragged by an ankle through town." I make a stop to grab a bottle of wine and a six-pack of PBR (proper gifts when visiting a writer), then head south into Paradise Valley where, on the east side of the Yellowstone River, tucked in the shadow of the Absaroka Mountains, is the "Grizfork," my cousin Doug Peacock's place, and a small writing cabin that will be my home for the next month.

Clyde crawls up the gravel road and swings into a spot in the tall grass between an aluminum canoe and an upside-down johnboat. I jump from the cab calling out the words of Whitman to the surrounding mountains and willows:

"Bearded, sun-burnt, gray-neck'd, forbidding, I have arrived."

interlude

Ahab Odysseus of the Hi-Line
claims to have traveled 9,000 miles
with Miscellaneous Jones
He claims that with each mile clocked
Jones read another line
from a book written in the hand
of Zorba Chaos himself
& Zorba claims the entire book
was transcribed directly from the words
of Moses Om

When Ahab raves about this
not a soul believes a damn thing he says

Yet there's no denying
when Ahab quotes Jones quoting Zorba quoting
Moses
a hush fills the room
& no one looks up from their drink
for a long, long time

Coastal Highway
second movement, reprise

Sweltering in the heat of late-summer El Paso in an upstairs apartment with pigeons always at the window, being not-rock doves and incessantly talking about the weather, I try to escape the sun's militant stomping. First I seek shelter in Ray's books – a cobbled-together shelf of Burroughs, Vonnegut and Bukowski in rummage-sale paperbacks. Then in my journal, scratching unfinished poems onto sweating pages that blur the ink like bad photos. Finally, in bottles of Tecate that are warm by the third drink. Nothing works – the devious heat discovers all my hiding places.

    I rolled in a few days ago after a midnight bus brought me from Colorado Springs to Albuquerque. On the way south from there, I stopped by White Sands, where I tried to look for birds but just saw atom bombs going off in negative everywhere I turned. When I first arrived at Ray's, we ordered a pizza since it's a universal truth that a pizza delivery guy will always have weed to sell. The universe, again, didn't lie.

Vagabond Song

We are halfway through the bag now, but it's too hot to be high. Instead it merely wraps us in the foam and polyester of a thousand disemboweled stuffed animals. Communication and movement are somewhat limited.

We rouse ourselves for a day trip to Juárez, but it's just the same heat with a louder soundtrack. The street hawks pull me apart, clawing for pesos. The pickups loaded with day workers spew thick exhaust into my eyes and lungs. Every horn in the known world is blasting into my head. We head back across the pedestrian bridge, where in the heat and pot haze, I can almost make out Williams' "form propped motionless … unrecognizable in the semi-dark."

Back at the apartment, night brings no relief. It's time to make a move. As Ray says, "Get the hell out of Dodge." Or in this case, dodge out of Hell.

"I guess I'll go to San Francisco."

"Why there?" asks Ray.

"A woman I met in Boulder said if I made it to the coast, I should look her up."

"Hook up?"

"No. Just to say hello."

Ray takes a last hit on a roach and drops the hemos into a hubcap ashtray. "Seems like a long way just to say hi," he says.

"True," I say, "but as Vonnegut says, 'Peculiar travel suggestions are dancing lessons from Dog.'"

"God?"

"Pot*ah*to."

I have a block of four free tickets from my brother, and rather than use up two to fly to Chicago and then to San Francisco, as they have no direct flights, I decide to just use one and go to Sacramento. Close enough.

Hitching out of an airport is tricky. Everyone's in a hurry, traffic is frenzied and the cops are on the lookout for anything or anyone that's out of place. After twenty minutes of being on the receiving end of suspicious glares, I spot my ride. Even though he's entering heavy traffic from three lanes away, it's a VW Thing – the driver *must* pick up hitchhikers (not to be confused with VW buses – those yuppie posers never pick you up). Almost causing an eleven-car pileup, the driver somehow breaks through the walls of honking, screeching madness and pulls over to me.

The kid at the wheel is about my age. Same build. Jacked up on life, high on the moment. He could be me. Yet I remember almost nothing. Not a word of conversation. Not a detail that separates him as a distinct personality from dozens of other rides. I remember his car. I remember it's a VW Thing.

The Thing drops me at a bus station, where I grab a shuttle over to San Francisco, home of Lawrence Ferlinghetti, who wrote, "A poem is a mirror walking down a strange street." Crossing the Bay Bridge feels like space flight. From a bulletin board at the station, I grab the address of a hostel and set out, one of the thousands of nomads who come to this city every day, most looking for the ghosts of Kerouac or Jerry Garcia. I'm just looking for a friendly woman from Long Island, met in Boulder, who reminds me of a young Barbra Streisand. But, more urgently, I'm looking for a drink.

Across the street from my hostel is the Black Magic Voodoo Lounge, a nice dive filled with New Orleans expats drinking Sazeracs and talking about the Saints' chances next season. I grab a cheap draft and put my quarters on the table. After a few games,

I'm up. It's a pretty even back and forth until I bank the 7, run the 3 long and kiss the 8 in the side (pardon my French). The Sandress at the Old Bar, Ma at Ewald's, Mato at Spike's Keg o' Nails and my brother at some Chicago joint (where we shot against some hillbillies on acid) have taught me well. Plus, there's something in the water of my hometown (aside from all the dioxins from Dow) that gives us certain abilities. People from Bay City, Michigan are better at pool than the national average. That's just a fact, like gravity or the Biogenetic Law of Recapitulation. Someone ought to write up a study on it for *Scientific American* or *Billiards Digest*.

I hold the table for three more games until the bartender takes her cue from its shiny black case.

"Rack 'em, Yankee," she says.

A thick shock of red hair falls over one eye as she lines up the break. A solid, immensely satisfying crack and she drops the 15 in the corner. She has a run of three more balls before I'm up. I slide some talc on my bridge hand, chalk up my 21, line up the shot ... and choke on an easy combo. Bay City blood, where have you gone?

Ontogeny recapitulates phylogeny. Yet another nice theory debunked.

She picks up the win and two more from regulars, who I can tell are used to losing to her. Then I'm back up. This time, luck, genetics, the stars and the blessing of St. Fats are with me and I squeak out a win. No one else is up so we decide to have a tiebreaker.

As I'm racking, she says, "You win this time and I'll buy you a drink."

"Sounds good," I say. "What if you win?"

"Then *you* buy you a drink."

I lift the rack and spin it back into its tray. "Sounds good either way."

She drops one of each on the break and then grabs the 4-ball. I sink the 9 in the side then the 11 in the corner, leaving the 15 a hiccup away from dropping. Mato always told me not to take my ducks, so instead I bring the 13 back then give in to the temptation of a scratch shot on the 10.

The bartender nabs a 7-2 combo, follows with the 2, then slices the 3.

"Nice shot."

"Thanks."

Her run continues with the 5 in the side, then she comes off the rail to drop the 6 in the corner. Things are looking grim as she eyes up the 8-ball.

"That's a lot of green," I tease.

"That's okay," she says. "I golf in my spare time."

Her shot looks good, but the 8 runs out of steam and stops just shy of the pocket.

"Damn!" she says. "Shoulda et my Wheaties today."

My work's cut out. No room for error or she'll have a cake with the 8. I've got to take my duck to get a position on the 10. I slam it hard and high and bring the potato back to the shallow end. The 10 drops without complaint, but the 8's blocking the easy shot on the 12. I'll have to bring it all the way back.

"That's a lot of green," she says.

"Yeah, and I hate golf," I say.

I stretch out across the table, one leg in the air behind me like a figure skater. I plant my bridge solidly and aim just below center. A soft clack and the 12 comes off the rail and rolls, rolls, rolls … and drops. I start breathing again and sink the 8 quickly, before I have a chance to over-think it.

It's closing time so she tosses me a wooden nickel.

"You got that drink coming whenever you want, Yankee."

"Thanks, Scarlett."

I figure I'll only be able to stay in town a couple of days since the hostel is twelve bucks a night. Hostels away from the big cities are usually only five to eight a night. These city digs are for the trustafarians or kids taking a gap year to "find themselves" before starting at Yale or Berkeley, depending on whether their parents are Republicans or Democrats. A nomad can only afford a brief stay before it's back on the road or the tracks or the trail where Mama Earth lets you crash for free.

But then I notice a sign on the message board offering a free bed in exchange for housekeeping. The desk clerk is happy to give me the job since otherwise she has to do it. So I begin my tenure as the live-in maid, like Mary Poppins without the umbrella, like Cinderella without the pumpkin, like Alice without the bowling trophies. Basically, an hour of cleaning two bathrooms and the kitchen each morning buys me a free, unlimited stay.

I have time to explore.

> The first time I saw the ocean
> was the first time the ocean saw me
>
> We were both surprised

I jump a local bus to see more of the city. Someone stops it at Haight Street so I hop off and begin walking west toward Golden Gate Park. I make my way through the hordes of tourists, deadheads and junkies. It's nearly impossible to tell which is which.

The tourists are in hippie costumes, the deadheads have eyes like junkies and the junkies move through the world like tourists at a shuttered amusement park. I soon slip into the shade of trees and shrubs that line the winding walkway of the park. Every third person I pass mutters a sales pitch: "Weed? Doses? Weed? Doses?" I'm tempted, but I figure the undercover cops are as indistinguishable from the tourists, deadheads and junkies as they are from each other.

    I spend hours meandering through arboretums and gardens, past fountains and hobo camps. Topping a small hill, I see a fenced enclosure holding two buffalo. I approach the chain link and watch as they pace back and forth. Same route. Same order. Back and forth. Over and over. They've worn a deep trench into the barren earth. I'm reminded of a water-tower mural spotted from a bus window on the road from Albuquerque to El Paso: Indians in chains being led by *conquistadores*, round and round the tower endlessly, frozen in eternal suffering just like the spirit of Unis-Ankh trapped in his statue at the Field Museum back in Chicago. The American theme. And this, here at the furthermost edge of the continent, is the culmination of the great crime called Manifest Destiny. This is the face of "progress." How the West was won.

Golden Gate Bison

    One billion hooves
    pounding the drum of the earth
    shaking rain from feral skies

    One billion bullets
    closing the eyes of stars
    writing the end of the song

Vagabond Song

> A young kid
> on his first trip to the ocean
> stands in the park watching two prisoners –
> two of the last of these furred gods –
> pace back & forth along the fenceline
> until the rut of their misery
> is two feet deep
>
> One billion hearts
> witness the slaughter
> then go back to their televisions

I leave them behind, feeling powerless, guilty. Knowing I've done my share of turning away.

Soon the world changes. I make my way through the last of the park, jog across the road and down the beach to stand, for the first time, at the edge of the ocean. Nothing could have prepared me for this.

It's the first glimpse of infinity, the first touch of boundless power. Wave after wave breaks into surf. Great rocks blast the water into towering plumes of salt spray filling the gull-shrieked air with a new music. My gaze follows the curve of the earth into absolute mystery.

> Roaring with bison-thunder
> The ocean & I
> Both hearts given to the moon

Two days later and I'm walking up Lombard, away from the section where it's the most crooked street on earth. On this section it's as straight as 87.2% of the world's streets. Through an open doorway, I hear my siren song – the clack of pool balls. There's no sign naming the bar, or even implying that it is a bar, but I tentatively step in to find a paneled room with a few dusty beer lights and an old guy sitting at the bar, a small dog snoozing under his stool. The bartender is reading the paper and a woman with long red nails and a mail-carrier uniform is shooting 8-ball with a retiree from an illusion factory. Most factories primarily produce illusions. Illusions of wealth, comfort, power, control, beauty, importance, status, happiness. As many illusions as it takes to ignore that persistent tapping at the door.

    I cross the room, slip onto a bar stool and order a scurvy special. The bartender introduces himself, then the rest of the gang: Bob, Vicki, Denny and Hamlet, "Ham" for short, who gives his tail a few sleepy wags at hearing his name. Just then the arm of the jukebox slides a new record from its nook and drops it onto the turntable. The initial crackle and static give way to the lonely and beautiful piano of Floyd Cramer, which tells the whole story in a handful of notes, followed by the desolate truth of the voice of Patsy Cline.

    I'm home. Again.

    This unnamed bar becomes part of my daily routine. After wandering the hills and streets of this haunted city, sometimes after winning and losing to Scarlett, the Voodoo bartender whose real name I never learn, I drop by this place to listen to Bob's stories until Vicki finishes her mail route. Then she and I shoot pool until the game comes on. On the day Bob gets his social security check, he buys rounds for the house until he's back to an equilibrium of contented poverty. Since he's doing shots and I'm having drafts, he's much faster than I so the bartender gives me wooden nickel drink tokens. I have a decent stack by the end of the night.

Vicki

Vicki slides into the bar like a snake takes to water
no ripple or sound
but right away she transforms the entire pool

Back-Alley Bob is propped at the bar
feeble dog tucked beneath his stool
tongue out, flop-eared & half blind
as another government check
changes itself into shots of whiskey

When Bob catches the scent
of her blood-red nails & raven hair
he becomes young again & in his drink
sees himself reflected, predatory & sharp

But then she moves away
to drop two quarters in the jukebox
& the image clouds
replaced by the stale, 80-proof blood
of a dying alcoholic

And then it happens: the last of my cash performs parlor magic, disappearing into a beer, and when I go to the money machine it sucks in my card and says, "Out of order, you commie scum!" or something to that effect. I spend a long weekend waiting for the bank to open, drinking Foster's at the docks with a one-armed Aussie who tells me about being taken up by aliens and hiking the Redwoods up north with an angry French nomad – he tries to buy us some acid on Haight Street, but it turns out to be nothing but bad-tasting paper. We hike all day through the colossal trees waiting for the trip to kick in. Eventually we arrive at the psychedelic ocean in time for the sunset, then hitch back to the city, exhausted, sullen and completely straight.

On Monday I visit the nice people at the bank, who nicely inform me that, yes, the machine wasn't working properly and it nicely ate my card, so they nicely mailed it back to my home bank, but just to be safe, they nicely cut it in half first. It would be a nice three weeks before I might get a replacement. Nice.

There's only one thing to do when you're broke: hit the road, Jack. So after a final night of cashing in all those wooden nickels at my neighborhood drinkeries, I play Jack to the road's Jill.

Miscellaneous Grass-Eatin' Far-Out Talkin' Blues

So I was in the park looking for a pigeon to feed
& this guy comes up to me & says,
What are you doing in California?
& I say I came to watch the sunrise
& he says, The sun doesn't rise here, it sets
& I say that's okay, I'll just stand on my head

But then all my money commits suicide
at that bar with no name – no, not a horse, a bar
I'm serious, it doesn't have a name
but it's at the corner of Lombard & Octavia
if you ever go there &
I figure it's better to be broke on the road
than broke in town
  so I say good-bye to Bob's dog
  & the one-armed Australian from outer space,
  pack my agoraphilia & leftover cheese
  & hit the road …

The first ride out of the city is a young couple high on love. They take me on a short stretch of the Coastal Highway, laughing with the beautiful thing that life has given them. Dog-damn, with all my heart I hope it will last.

Vagabond Song

> ... & I'm out there with Woody & Willie &
>   Bob & Red
> Phaedrus & Ford & Pretty Boy Floyd
> & I wish they'd stop singin' & strummin'
>   & harpin' & hummin'
> & philosophyin' & prophecyin' &
>   harmonizin' & alphabetizin'
> & get the hell out of my head
> I mean I love 'em all
> but I need my own tune on my own road
> under my own sky
> waitin' for my own ride & when it comes
> it'll be my thumb that reels it in
> bug-eyed & gapin' like a hooked fish ...

A shirtless, spike-haired guy picks me up in an open-air Jeep. His skin is inked with skulls and snakes and words too pale to read. As soon as we're up to speed, well past the limit, he says, "Sorry if I'm driving too fucking fast, but I just got out of prison and found out that my girlfriend dumped me and my best friend killed himself."

I have no response.

We race on in tense silence. He's on a trip of absolute destruction, seething with anger at the world. I'm convinced that I'll soon be dead. But then he lays off the accelerator and we slow to a relaxed coast.

"I'm sorry, man," he says. "I don't mean to freak you out. I'm just having a really bad day."

> ... & then it comes ...

> Another ramblin' pickup
> & let me tell all you young neo-hippy punks
> don't you for one minute think
> that guys in trucks are assholes like I used to think

>
> cuz when you're out there hitchin'
> you'll get more rides from pickups
> than all other vehicles combined
> I mean, don't even bother with VW buses
> Shit, if I had a nickel
> for every time a microbus passed by
> without a glance
> I wouldn't be tellin' on this tale
> I'd hire someone else to tell it for me,
>   ya know what I mean?
> All I'm sayin' is all you bus-drivin' yuppie posers
> are rackin' up some kind of bad-ass karma
> Brothers & sisters, pity the Birkenstock,
>   tie-dyed wannabes
> for they shall be disinherited from the
>   kingdom of goddess
> OM MANI PADME HUM
>   AMEN
>   HARE KRISHNA
>   YAHOO! ...

The next guy reminisces about his hitchhiking days after Vietnam. I can hear the regret in his voice that his life is no longer marked by days of the road's freedom. He drops me at a gas station, where I lean my pack against the brick wall and hit the john. When I come back out, there's two bottles of beer resting on my pack. He might no longer be a vagabond, but he's still an angel. As is the guy who hands me a business card, saying, "Drop me a postcard sometime." Folded underneath is a twenty-dollar bill.

> ... My boot scrapes the gravel
> like the ringin' of an inside-out bell
> as I hop into the cab
> & this guy's old & weathered
> like an iron rooster on top of some barn

> but his eyes are young
> & that's what really counts
> I've seen kids with ancient eyes
> like they've already seen too much
> & could close them right now & never miss the light
> but not this guy ...

The next ride takes me to Monterey. For six bucks I sleep on the floor of the high school gym with two dozen other nomads, gypsies, travelers, pilgrims, migrants, hobos, angels, peregrines, vagabonds and takers of the road less traveled. In the morning, I head down to the bus stop and ask a driver which bus will get me to a good place to continue hitching down the magic of the coast. Swear to Dog, and I would never lie about such a thing, he says, "You want to take the Number 4 ... out to a place called the Crossroads."

> ... & as we roll along
> w/ the mountains whisperin' in my left ear
> & the sea's got a-hold of my right
> his voice sounds like a little of both
> when he says, So whaddaya do?
> & I say I write
> & he says, Write?
> & I say yeah
> & he says, Any money in that?
> & I say what difference does it make?
> & he says, Well, you gotta eat ...

Another ride and another ride and I'm dropped off on the roadside, but something's different.

What is this place?

"Big Sur," answers a sign on a wooden post.

I walk. There's magic here. It's overwhelming. The sea is an invisible presence far below cliffs that are themselves hidden by sun-dappled redwoods. The air is charged as if the world's greatest thunderstorm has just passed. Each breath is electric. I don't even know (at the time) about the connection with Jack Kerouac and Henry Miller and Aldous Huxley. This place, in and of itself, has power – no human influence is needed. Three cars pull over and offer a ride. Three times I decline, content to keep walking.

Eventually a rambling pickup slides alongside me and a door swings open. I hop in. The guy's old and worn, reminds me of a weather vane creaking in the languid breeze of summer. But his eyes are young.

> ... & I sit back & I think about that
> I look at the mountains
> I look at the sea
> I look down at my anxious boots
> & then I look straight down the center
> of that asphalt two-lane scream & say
>
> If there's no money to buy my food
> I'll go outside & eat the grass
> If there's no grass
> I'll fast
> until it grows

He takes me to the next ride, the next poem. The days merge into one Great Day. A day in some summer of youth when the sun tumbles light from rainless skies and time holds still just long enough to touch freedom. The road unfurls in unbounded possibility. Miles pass like birds on an endless migration. For as long as I can, I'll fly with them.

coda: THE GRIZFORK

I'VE SETTLED IN, off the road. At least for a while.

After a mad run with Bashō, a Jeepster for your love, across the silence of North Dakota and the quickening of Eastern Montana – a nonstop grinding from Minneapolis to Livingston, I tack upstream along the Yellowstone then cut to the foot of the Absarokas to the Grizfork, home of Doug Peacock, who wrote, "The best wisdom comes directly from the Earth. It runs right up our roots into the spirit. Walk on. The feet will inform the soul."

I have a small writing cabin here. A ramshackle, one-room, pine-scented, snow draped, windswept, handcrafted, sun-washed, moss-spackled, mountain man's cabin. A book-lined, cloud-hidden, candlelit, Han Shanic, willow-shaded, rain-battered, roughhewn, outlaw, shoebox cabin. A Waldenesque, coyote-circled, timeworn, wine-stained, satori-seeking, bird-gathering, history-whispering, snowmelt-dripping, tempest-tossed, typewriter-echoing cabin.

It's a good place to be still and watch the transit of clouds, the

round dance of the seasons. It's a good place to drop my pack and allow some roots to grow. As Miscellaneous Jones says, "A tree without roots is just a log. Firewood."
    It's time to dig in.
    Off the road.
    At least for a while.

Writing at Grizfork Studio (*Pica Hudsonia*)

Each day begins
with the conversations of magpies
who never run out of things to talk about

Each morning unfolds
with the fact of those mountains
who never feel the need to say a thing

I sit at my desk
with both & try to grab hold
of what lies between the two

On a good day
I come close

Casa Parota
bonus track #1

WAVES BLAST THE BOW OF THE *PANGA* immediately after departing from Muelle de los Muertos, "pier of the dead" – a name too obvious to take as an omen – but now, with the sea a swelling gray beast lashing at us with salt-sharpened claws as we grip our open wooden benches, perhaps not. Our captain does an expert job of keeping us pointed into the waves so, though we rise and fall nearly a dozen feet, the risk of capsizing is kept relatively low. Yet the sea and the wind continue their tricks, and every few minutes a rogue wave knocks us askew, the jungle-clad coastline disappears, and "los muertos" is heard in the screeching of circling gulls.

> In the screams of gulls
> *los muertos, los muertos,* yet
> this still is music

But death will have to go home empty-handed as we finally

Vagabond Song

round a point of pelican-dotted rocks and motor into the slightly milder cove of the village. We pry our hands free of the boat's benches and leap to the timeworn dock where our host waits to take us up the narrow cobblestone paths and steep winding steps to our rooftop home in the singing jungle.

> Casa Parota
> Lulled to sleep by the surf
> Awakened by birds
>
> Chachalacas & roosters
> Collared doves & kiskadees
>
> Yellow-winged caciques
> gathering the morning light
> to build teardrop nests
>
> Black vultures & frigatebirds
> trade places in the mottled sky

The days begin with good, strong coffee on our terrace overlooking the forest of parota, bamboo and palm trees, down to the rooftops of the village, red Spanish tile and chalk white concrete dotted with water tanks, and the dome of the church rising silent above the music of life, the syncopated drumbeat of *la gente*. The street dogs know that god is in the mud and muck of the feral, never within the walls of dogma. Halfway around the world, a genocide is raging in the name of the god of walls. The same god whose walls divide as well as enclose. My complicity is inescapable even here.

> Patio carpet
> Red flowers & yellow leaves
> of the tulip tree

> I have tried to stop war but
> I didn't try very hard
>
> Sweeping the morning's leaves
> one jumps before my broom & flies
> back to its butterfly life
>
> An accordion drifts through the palms
> The birds don't care that it's Easter

I take a Bashō-reading nap, drifting from his impressions on the narrow road to my dream-images and scraps of thought moving like cirrus streaks across the blue-gray field of memory, and back again, with the caciques and roosters and distant street dogs adding their voices and now, back at this table on the terrace with a Modelo and my binoculars in case the trogons come back.

Hiking through a jungle of Orange-fronted Parakeets, Military Macaws and Elegant Trogons. A jungle of resistance and defiance. A fortress against the utter destruction of so-called development, against the savagery of so-called luxury resorts. The Wixárika (Huichol) People, have so far managed to hold the forces at bay – mostly by not allowing a road to reach their village. No road means no cars, and no cars means everything.

> At the waterfall
> Anointment & renewal
> In the blast of life

After a swim and blessing in the cascading waters, we hike the trail that echoes the Tuito River back down to the village, where we hit our regular *tienda* for tortillas, beans, platanos and cerveza for dinner back at our rooftop casita. A few more days of this magical place. A few more pages of this journal. A few more

Vagabond Song

sweepings of fallen tulip flowers on the concrete terrace.

    As the sun drops lower and softer in the Western sky, a loose flock of travelers waits at the pier for the panga back to the city. Tomorrow we will join them and leave behind these birdsongs and falling flowers.

> Early evening sea
> plays arpeggios on the fishing boats
> splayed across the cove
>
> Little house lizard here's a feast of ants
> Come dine while I finish this last page
>
> The moon in my door
> but an ocean away from
> Bashō's fragrant plums
>
> Winter still holds my far home
> A stranger waiting in shadow

interlude

Miscellaneous Jones hasn't been seen
in a long damn time
It's getting so most people you meet
have never heard of him

Those that remember look away
when they hear the name

Some say he's hopped a freighter
to the South China Sea
Some say he's deep in a cave
high in the Andes

Some say he's still around, just laying low
Some say he was never here at all

But the one thing we really know
is this cold old world
Needs him now
more than ever before

THE HUNDRED HIGHWAYS TOUR
bonus track #2

[*Ten years ago, in support of* Vagabond Song, *I embarked on the "Hundred Highways Tour," traveling 100 highways to visit bookstores, bars, libraries, festivals, restaurants, coffeehouses, galleries and anywhere else they'd have me, to share my stories with new friends and fellow travelers. Sometimes alone, sometimes with others, always with my ragged, gig case, plastered with stickers – an old green suitcase I rescued from a thrift store dumpster back in Saginaw, Michigan.*

These reports from the road began as blog posts on CrowVoice.com. *The original versions, with photos, are still there, if you can find them. Several of the poems became part of my book,* Life List.

A careful reader might notice some highway numbers repeated, but I only counted them toward the total when I was traveling a different stretch of the highway in question. In reality, all roads are one, and it always leads to the next poem if we're really paying attention, remaining open and listening with everything we've got.]

Vagabond Song

#1: US Route 89 to Elk River Books

THE BACKBONE OF THE ROCKIES, aka the National Park Highway – connecting seven of them as it rolls its way from Arizona to the Canadian border – U.S. Route 89 is the first of 100 highways on the tour for *Vagabond Song*. We kick it all off with the book launch party on Sept. 3, 2015, at Elk River Books, at the time a half-block from Park St., the highway's alias as it slides through town. The event is a good old revelry of Dionysian shade. A great gathering of Livingston comrades. Edd Enders discusses the artwork he provided for the book, noting our mutual respect for and inspiration from the same beings: crows, trees and open roads. My cousin Doug Peacock gives me a beautiful intro, telling the story of the two of us mucking around the swamps of Shiawassee Flats back in Michigan to repatriate arrowheads and spear points gathered in his youth. The room is packed, the wine flowing like the Yellowstone in spring, and the journey begins: travelling 100 highways to share this new critter of a book at bookstores and bars, libraries and museums, restaurants and festivals. To go looking, again after so many years, for those Vagabond Angels who must still be out there. Somewhere. Waiting for their poem.

#2 – 4: MT-10W, I-90 & Route 191 to Imagine Butte Resource Center

I'VE BEEN INVITED TO READ at a humming hive of creative energy, the Imagine Butte Resource Center. Unfortunately, to get from Livingston to Butte, the route options are pretty much limited to I-90 due to the several mountain passes you need to traverse. One of our country's *unfreeways*. However, during the first stretch, I-90 is concurrent with U.S. Route 191, a great border-to-border ribbon from Douglas, Arizona to Loring, Montana, with a brief respite in Yellowstone National Park, where I was gifted this moment:

> Yellowstone raven
> holds fast to wind-dancing spruce
> Eye of every storm

I like Butte. It has the same energy and edge of many Midwestern towns that have also been built, chewed up, poisoned and abandoned by industry. It's the standard process of transforming the raw materials of earth and humans into money. But the humans who survive, like weeds that crack the concrete, create some of my favorite art. I've seen it in Detroit and Saginaw and Flint. I see it again in this city where the IWW's Frank Little was (as his gravestone attests) "slain by capitalist interests for organizing and inspiring his fellow men."

The folks at Imagine Butte are whipping up a whirlwind of creative activity just up the street from the Berkeley Pit, an open pit mine turned toxic lake – "waters 900 feet deep / acidic enough to dissolve a boat" (from "Progress" published in *Life List*) – and maybe because of that, they are passionate when talk turns to the environmental destruction threatened by proposed gold mines just north of Yellowstone.

The audience-driven discussion reminds me of why I write. Or maybe not "why" – the answer to that question is the same as "why do I breathe?" or "why does my blood flow" – but rather, "what is the value of writing?" We're in a time that every artist needs to stay engaged in the Struggle. There's no time left for the self-absorbed "look-at-me, look-at-me, look-at-me" artists. We need artists who are warriors. Blissful, wild revolutionaries and

Vagabond Song

mad saints with knife-sharp pens and brushes. With machine-gun typewriters.

I hope to meet more of these poets of resistance on these 100 highways. I hope you, too, are busy sharpening your pen.

#5, 6: Route 12 & MT-1 to the Montana Book Festival

FROM BUTTE ONWARD, to the Montana Book Festival in Missoula for a reading at Shakespeare & Co., named for the legendary Paris bookshop that published *Ulysses* and changed the world forever. I share the stage (and a fantastic Sauvignon Blanc from Régis Minet before the reading) with Gary Whited, one of those really fine, gentleman poets who remind me that I need to work harder and dig deeper with my own poetry. From his collection, *Having Listened*, he hooks me with the line: "Meadowlark on barbed wire, yellow breasted door opens with its song."

The night comes to an end sitting in a 5th floor windowsill listening to a shadowed stranger playing a street piano.

> Piano player
> taps stars into the night sky
> Nocturnal nocturne

On the way home, we take MT Hwy 1, the Pintler Scenic Route, a relaxing cruise through towns like Hall and Maxville and on into Philipsburg to enjoy the elixirs offered by the local brew pub and catch a fiery bad-ass down-home blues set by a band called Smokestack & the Foothill Fury. Montana has some of the best band names I've heard: Little Jane & the Pistol Whips, Two-story Ranch, The Thirty-aught Hicks, Doublewide Dreams, Laney Lou & the Bird Dogs, the Kitchen Dwellers, The Bus Driver

The Hundred Highways Tour

Tour, and my own brief project, Remington Streamliner – named for "Moonstar," the typewriter that *Vagabond Song* opens with.

As it nears its terminus, folding back into I-90, Highway 1 rolls through Anaconda and Opportunity, past the Anaconda Smelter Stack. This 585-foot-tall structure, capable when it was in use, of spewing out three to four million cubic feet per minute of toxic gas, is the tallest free standing masonry structure in the world. The Washington Monument could fit inside it. That's about the best metaphor for American capitalism I can imagine.

#7: MT-86 to Country Bookshelf

WE HAVE TO GET A LITTLE CREATIVE for our route to Bozeman to avoid, yet again, traveling the same stretch of I-90. So we head up to Clyde Park and take the breathtakingly scenic Brackett Creek Rd. to Highway 86 which hugs the south-eastern front of the Bridger Mountains.

It's worth the extra time. As always, "making good time" should refer to quality not quantity.

Brackett Creek (*Aquila chrysaetos*)

> Gold coins of aspen shimmer on hillsides
> as a Golden Eagle lifts from a fence post
>
> follows the slope of the land like notes
> undulating across a sheet of music
>
> Some adagio written late in the composer's life
> returning to a major key for the first time in years
>
> Sunlight painting spruces, barns & the ribboning road
> unrolling before us like our best possible future

surrounded by the only gold that isn't fool's gold
we drive into the promise of love

#8: MT-3 to the High Plains Bookfest

BOOK FESTIVALS ARE GREAT REMINDERS of the importance of community in the writing world. We spend so much of our time alone, plucking away at a typewriter or scratching the pages of a journal, accompanied by a cold cup of coffee and a snoring cat. Not many people understand what it is we're doing, or why. Often, neither do we. Writing is wandering a dark cave with a dim flashlight. Something fantastic is painted on the walls, but we can only make out a bit at a time. We must, from time to time, head back to the surface and compare notes with other explorers with their own dim flashlights. Not only to expand the understanding of the picture, but to recharge our batteries so we can head back down with a brighter light. So an opportunity to gather writers and readers together, to celebrate the books that move us, change us and challenge us, to hear our words spoken aloud and echoing off other souls, is vital to the continuance of our craft.

I check into my room at the Dude Rancher, with its carpet of cattle brands and matching headboard, then bolt over to the Visible Vault to read a couple poems and be a judge for a terrific poetry slam. I used to do a lot of slam poetry back in the Midwest and it's been a while since I've attended an event with this much talent. It reminds me of the energy back at the Kraftbrau in Kalamazoo. There the wild poems flowed as freely as the beer, and I met some damn fine writers and comrades.

The next night, I meet up with some other poets at a weekly jazz jam at the Yellowstone Valley Brewing Co. Garage and dog-damn! I had no idea there was such a great jazz scene in Montana. Really hot players, good cold beer. I'm invited up to perform a poem with the band. I do a new piece, "*Adundo donax*," from a work-in-progress that contrasts the positive beauty and power of John Coltrane with the ugly death-wish of the Coal Train.

My reading for the festival itself is a perfect example of the community of writers and its value, sharing the lectern (which is not a podium) with poets Tami Haaland, Cara Chamberlin, Dave Caserio and Nathan Petterson. Hearing their words definitely reveals more of the cave painting and serves to recharge the batteries. And now, with those recharged batteries, I'm ready to head back down into the cave. There's another poem down there, waiting to be brought to light.

#9, 10: US-87 & MT-208 to Cassiopeia Books

THIS IS THE KIND OF DRIVE that roads were invented for: Highway 89 through Clyde Park, Wilsall, Ringling and White Sulphur Springs before plunging into the Little Belt Mountains and the Lewis & Clark National Forest. An unrolling canvas of fall colors and streams reflecting a riot of sunlight is accented by golems of limestone rising from road's edge into the sapphire sky.

We stop off in Niehart (pop. 51/elev. 5661') for a cold road drink at Bob's Bar. The marquee reads "NEXT BEER STOP 57 MILES" – how could I not pull over? Friendly folks and classic small-town-bar atmosphere. Unfortunately, no time for a game of pool, I've got a reading to get to.

So onward to US-87 and MT-208, from Belt to Great Falls. We check into the historic Hotel Arvon (a suite for the price of a broom-closet), and head over to the bookstore. Cassiopeia Books is a gem of a place in a city suffering the bad karma of its proximity to Malmstrom Air Force Base with its Minuteman missiles

Vagabond Song

waiting to wipe out humanity. Rich book selection, funky location, fantastic crowd, and Andrew, the owner, is the righteous heart of it all. A good bookstore is the best way to negate the evils of the military/industrial complex.

Of course, the night must end at the other gem of this town: The Sip 'n Dip Tiki Lounge, with mermaids swimming behind the bar.

>   Poetry & mermaids
>   while the missiles sleep in their silos
>   dreaming of children
>   turned to ash
>
>   A man sits between
>   a phone & a button thumbing
>   through a tattered secondhand book
>   & hums a lullaby

#11 – 19: MT-2, US-287, MT-87, US-20, I-15, US-30, ID-34, US-91 & I-84 to Ken Sanders Rare Books

ONWARD TO KEN SANDERS' LEGENDARY BOOKSHOP in Salt Lake for the second time. I read here years ago with my cousin Doug Peacock and have been anxious to have a new book and so a reason to come back.

Rolling through the lonesome beauty of southwestern Montana and eastern Idaho, I watch a dozen antelope lope single file toward the shadow of snow-shrouded mountains, then a cloud of pelicans rising from a riverbank. The road snakes between rock walls and echoes glittering streams before spilling out into Pocatello.

Meanwhile (*Pelecanus erythrorhynchos*)

Lifting like a fog
from the face of the river
wings torment the air

as a single line of pronghorn
lope into the shadow
of Cinnamon Mountain

the pelicans paint themselves
across the marbled sky yet somehow
    somewhere
we are still bombing children

We arrive in SLC the next afternoon. A circle of old friends gathers around the music of poetry and story. A small crowd for a reading, but a perfect size for good conversation. After the reading, Ken, Lisa & I polish off the last of the wine and head to a nouveau speakeasy, hidden in the basement of a taco joint. Ken makes a quick phone call. A few minutes later an unmarked steel door opens and we are escorted down a dark flight of stairs into another time. Fantastic food and drinks and music and art and celebration and libation and inebriation and bizarre taxidermy watching over it all. We end up at Ken's "Forest House," another fantastical spot concealed in a wrinkle on the map. Through the Doc Sarvis gate into the enchanted garden. In my mind, this place is the real temple of this town. That quartz-monzonite behemoth downtown is far too garish and opulent to house any kind of deity that I would care to know. I like my deities like I like my crash pads: rough around the edges, down-to-earth and surrounded by trees.

The next day, we head north, entering the town of West Yellowstone in such a thick fog that the place is invisible until the last moment. Someone throws a switch and a town appears. Time for a road drink. In this case, a Good Medicine Red Ale at the Slippery Otter. And then we are off, climbing 191 as it flirts with the border of Yellowstone Park and chases the Gallatin River back to the interstate.

#20, 21: MT S-205 & M-13 to Bradley's Bistro

BACK TO THE OLD HOMELAND of Saginaw, Michigan for a gig at a friend's restaurant. I read some of the Saginaw-based excerpts from *Vagabond Song* and am struck by the changes since my early days here. Although there are still far too many "burned-out houses and boarded-up liquor stores ... vacant lots of broken glass and the rusted skeletons of industry," it occurs to me that this space where I'm reading and enjoying great food, wine and friendship, probably had been one of those boarded up and forgotten buildings. Now, with new windows and a new life, artwork by several old friends covering the walls, and laughter filling the air, the space is a beacon of hope for this tired old town.

#22 – 25: Northern, Western, Hummingbird & Southern Highways to Miss Bertie's Community Library

A COUPLE DAYS AFTER CHRISTMAS, we fly to Belize and jump into a van that takes us, three hours later, to Hopkins Village on the Caribbean coast. The drive introduces me to my favorite name for a road: The Hummingbird Highway. It's an adventure of potholes, jungle-clad mountains, "sleeping policemen" (the ubiquitous, teeth-shattering speedbumps that are the only method of getting locals to slow down), and an unending narrative of jokes,

The Hundred Highways Tour

history, puns and legends from our driver, all accompanied by a few bottles of Belikin Beer.

I don't have a reading here, but Dianne has me sign a copy of the book that I donate to Miss Bertie's Community Library, so I'm counting it. My tour – my rules.

This wonderful little gem of books was created by Miss Bertie, a Peace Corps volunteer in 2007, and has been serving both the children and adults of Hopkins ever since. It's wonderful to visit and see the single room building full of kids discovering new worlds within the pages of the mostly donated books. A library is the heart of a community. A communal gathering place where people become stronger, freer and more empathetic. Where life can take on new vistas, horizons can be rendered boundless.

The next day, we're floating an underground river in St. Herman's Cave. Descending into *Xibalba*, the Mayan Underworld, the flickering of bats, the crystal-clear water. I stop below a shower dripping from a stalactite and allow the holy water to wash over my face. Vida, our guide, notices and says, "Getting a good Mayan blessing, huh?" He knows exactly what I'm up to.

In the rainforest along the Monkey River, with Howler Monkeys filling the air with their mad whooping, I resist the temptation of wander off from the group and become a little creature of the jungle. Maybe a Jaguarundi or a Paca, the "royal rat." The immensity of green, the water-soaked air, and the glittering of sunlight through 20-foot leaves cast their spell. I am spell-bound. It takes several weeks for the charm to wear off, if it really has.

Vagabond Song

New Year's Eve at the Swinging Armadillo
(*Quiscalus mexicanus*)

Great-tailed Grackle grips
a power line crossing overhead
The year is ending by certain clocks

By others, tonight is just another night
His bluegreenpurpleblack plumage
like the sea where the ship of days

sinks into myth, fades
into unreliable memories &
nothing can hold out against the deep

At this bar at the edge of town,
where "Hopkins Village" is shed
in favor of its old name, Yugadan,

a half-moon rises from the sea:
bowl of oranges & black flowers
on a tablecloth of stars

Garifuna drummers pound out
the final moments of my year
I too, have been stretched taut enough to echo

Soon winter will feel again like winter
but for now, all is music & moonlight
& the waves unfold on the dock like orchids

#26 – 34: I-90, MT-84, US-191, US-20, I-15, MT-41, MT-287, MT-55 & MT-2 to King's English Bookshop

MY THIRD VISIT TO SALT LAKE CITY, but my first visit to the lake itself. There's something quietly unsettling about a lake with no fish. Other than brine shrimp, brine flies, algae and bacteria, nothing lives in these waters, nothing else can survive. Just knowing that makes standing at its shore disorienting. It's stunningly beautiful, but it's an otherworldly beauty – lunar, alien.

And deadly.

As climate change dries the surrounding land and a growing population diverts more and more water otherwise destined for it, the lake is disappearing before our eyes. As it turns to dust, high levels of trapped mercury blow into the city, poisoning the people. The same people who are taking the water that, had it been allowed to replenish the lake, would have prevented the toxic dust from developing. The same mercury is moving up the food chain, from brine shrimp to ducks to the hunter feeding his family. Strands of the Web. It's impossible to cut one strand without feeling the vibrations throughout the entire, interwoven structure.

> When the lake becomes dust
> & the dust enters the rivers of our blood
> no fish will swim through our bodies
> no birds will fly through our dreams
>
> When the lake becomes dust
> & the dust chokes our last breath
> no songs will leave our lips
> no prayers will reach the sky

#35, 36: I-90 & US-12 to Fact and Fiction Books

WE PLAN ON TAKING BACK ROADS, maybe 141 to 200 so we could pass through Avon and Ovando, or maybe 1 to 38 to 93 to find road drinks in Porters Corner or Victor. But by the time we get out the door, we have just enough time to race on the interstate unfreeway, straight to our hotel in Missoula, a block away from the gig at Fact & Fiction.

We arrive with a few minutes to spare. Enough to run across the street to grab two bottles of wine to share with the small but friendly crowd. One of the wines is named "Duct Tape" and tastes as bad as it sounds. But I have to get it anyway, in honor of the line from my poem "M-46, October":

> Clyde's old diesel rolls to a wary stop
> & I hop from the cab
> onto a protest of gravel
> beneath my duct-taped boots

Fact & Fiction is a great reminder of how vital our local independents bookshops are. The shelves are packed with titles that go much deeper than the generic reads of box stores or malls. "Local Author" tags protrude from everywhere. Barbara and Mara are more than welcoming and, as with indie shops across the country, I feel at home. All those local author signs represent the important bond between writers and bookstores – both need the other to thrive. As a writer, I can't say enough about booksellers who support writers. As a bookseller, I can't say enough about the authors who support my shop.

#37 – 41: US-93, MT-200, MT Secondary 471, NF-9, I-90 to The Well-Read Moose

SINCE MY READING THE NIGHT BEFORE was followed by some serious barhopping, we get a late start to Coeur d'Alene for my next gig. But we are still able to take backroads. Cutting north on 93, passing near the Garden of One Thousand Buddhas and noticing numerous road signs in the Salish and Kootenai languages. Their alphabets use characters and symbols far beyond my understanding, but the English translations are fantastic: "Place Where You

Surround Something" and "Little Valley Behind Hills."

After a road drink in Thompson Falls, we cross a mountain pass that throws us back into winter. The Midwesterner in me still has trouble fathoming severe snow and ice conditions in April, but we get lucky and are able to make it through, dropping into Idaho and back into spring.

Thompson Pass (*Meleagris gallopavo*)

Let's begin the day
listening to Brahms
in a Missoula hotel room then

the drive along the spring roiling
of the Flathead River
with tongues of fog

lolling up from mouths
of fir trees tasting the sky
Let's stop at a bar in Thompson

Falls for a pint & to find
out if the pass is open –
snow & rain & a Wild Turkey

at the roadside like a hitchhiker
but drivable if we take it slow –
& the confusion of west-

flowing rivers in place of
my habitual eastbound ones
Yesterday, a coyote

on the median testing
the limits of mortality &
the physics of steel. Tomorrow

> a dark corner bar in Spokane
> with bad music & too many TVs
> But today, as soaring as
>
> the Brahms as delicate as the
> fog, to be here with the woman
> I love with bellies full
>
> of sushi & the lights of Coeur
> d'Alene seeping through the blinds
> & painting our bodies in joy

#42, 43: I-90 & US-2 to the GetLit! Festival

A SHORT HOP FROM COEUR D'ALENE to Spokane for the GetLit! Fest. Too much free wine, too fancy of a hotel, and a fantastic downtown and park. Mostly I walk around being surprised by how nice of a city this is. I'd only visited once before, and that was just long enough to fill a U-Haul truck with boxes of cousin Doug's book, *Walking It Off*. The press that had published it was getting the axe by the university, so we bought up all their stock. The trip was too quick to see a thing.

So it's great to be able to spend a few days here. After my reading and teaching a playwriting workshop, someone asks me if I'd been to the waterfall yet. I'd seen signs for it in the park and for some reason pictured a small run of whitewater cascading over rocks, maybe a couple dozen yards worth of drop – pretty, but not a huge priority.

Why that was my assumption, I have no idea. I'd forgotten the importance of remaining open to everything while on the road (or anywhere for that matter). With a deafening roar and 100' drop, misting water catching beams of sunlight through the arches of the bridges, the falls are among the most beauti-

The Hundred Highways Tour

ful I've seen. Definitely a huge priority. Anytime someone says, "You should go see this," it's vital to remember the words of Kurt Vonnegut: "Peculiar travel suggestions are dancing lessons from God."

#44 – 47: M-25, I-75, I-23, M-14 to Bookbound

OVER 30 YEARS AGO, Ann Arbor was my first awakening to a much bigger and more interesting world. Social and political activism learned at the anti-apartheid protests in the Diag. Being overwhelmed by the sheer expansiveness of what there was to be known while wandering the labyrinth of shelves at the grad library. Getting hip to the wonders of mind- and sense-expanding substances in the form of a baggie of Pinconning Paralyzer in a dorm room of Mary Markley Hall. At the time, I was a student at a small college in a mid-Michigan cornfield. My best friend was a student here, and in my Freshmen year, I visited every weekend I could. I was the poor kid who wanted to transfer to U of M but knew I could never afford to. Ann Arbor was my Christminster.

This was also where I discovered and fell head over teabag for independent bookstores. Magical places like Shaman Drum, West Side Bookshop, Wooden Spoon Books, Crazy Wisdom, Dawn Treader, David's Books, and the original Borders – before they sold out to Kmart and the corporate suits did what they always do to any cultural institution they touch.

And now, these long decades later, I have the pleasure of reading at a new arrival in the long line of soul-preserving shops, Bookbound. The owners, Peter and Megan, are fantastically welcoming. The crowd is small but a great chance to reunite with some old friends, including the damn fine poet Monica Rico, one of our Saginistas from the Old Town Saginaw poetry, music and

Vagabond Song

art scene back in the day.

After the reading, drinks and more drinks with great friends, old and new. The next day, I make pilgrimages to the old bookshops that have survived the Amazon wars, and kick around the art fair, where I buy a new hat, just in time to wear for my next gig.

#48, 49: M-13 & M-84 to Bemo's Bar

NO TOUR IS COMPLETE WITHOUT A VISIT to my hometown of Bay City, Michigan and a gig at Bemo's, my favorite Bay City bar (now that the Old Bar is long gone). The show is a fantastic gathering of friends and family, including my brother and comrade Todd Berner who opens with a set of his damn good songs.

The absolute highlight of the evening (or maybe the entire tour) is sitting in during the Northwoods Improvisers set who closed out the night after my feature. These cats (Mike Johnston, Mike Gilmore, and Nick Ashton) inspire me like few other living musicians do. It's an honor to introduce their music to some new people, and then to share a new poem paired with their take on Alice Coltrane's "Prima":

Communion

"All a musician can do
is to get closer to the sources of nature,
and so feel that he is in communion
with the natural laws."
– John Coltrane
spoke these words, 1962
the same year Eichmann's ashes are scattered
on the Mediterranean to be absorbed by plankton
which is eaten by crustaceans,
climbing up the food chain to eventually become

the fish eaten by millions during Passover Seders &
300 people die in Germany's largest coal mine explosion &
in Pennsylvania, a coal fire begins burning,
decimates two towns & will continue burning
for 250 more years & Bob Dylan
first sings "A Hard Rain's a-Gonna Fall"
& 55 years later
I sit outside this bar
in a brief respite between coal trains
listening to the sparrows
discuss a coming storm
the aspens of the courtyard
sighing their thirst, soon to be sated

All any of us can do
    (as the first rain drops fall)
is to get closer to the sources of nature
    (as the birds fall silent)
& so feel we are in communion
w/ the natural laws
    (even though what I first take for thunder
    is instead the next coal train
    rounding the bend)

#50 – 52: US-287, US-12 & MT-284 to Bedrock Books

NORTH ON 287 WITH WHEAT AND ALFALFA running like ponies across the rolling expanse bound for the mountains on every horizon. It's one of those late-summer days that poets keep trying to capture in words but never do. It's one of those big sky days that gives a state its nickname. I almost regret that I have a reading to get to: it would be fantastic to just keep driving, letting the roads unroll wherever they wish, only stopping for gas in towns I've never heard of.

But Helena pulls me in just in time to check into my room and head over to Bill's house for a memorable dinner of chicken saltimbocca and a great malbec in a gorgeous backyard with Bantams roaming the underbrush and hummingbirds making the air vibrate with life.

Bill is the owner of Bedrock Books, where my reading is being held. But first, the writer and musician Aaron Parrett and I swing by his place to pick up a banjo and have a look at his book collection. We geek out on James Joyce for a while, which isn't something you can do with most banjo players. Only the best of them.

The reading at Bedrock is like a house concert: a comfy living room full of new friends, surrounded by beautiful books, good beer in the fridge and afterwards, a gathering in the backyard with night sounds, drunk neighbors and good stories passed around the circle. And I think, Oh yeah, that's why I do this! Why I drive long hours to sell a few books. It's these moments of fantastic people and places that open themselves to an out-of-town poet and say, "Hey, let me tell you a story."

#53, 54: US-89 & Highway 540 to Pine Creek

PINE CREEK IS THE FIRST PLACE I PERFORMED when first moving to Montana. I was asked to open for a band called the Fossils, for which I wrote my poem called "Fossils." That began a great stretch of readings, and performances including the debut of Remington Streamliner, the defunct poetry band that lasted about as long as poetry bands do.

More importantly, Pine Creek has a place in history as having been home base, for a time, of the Montana Gang, a loose group of writers, artists, actors and musicians that included Richard Brautigan, Tom McGuane, Jim Harrison, Gatz Hjortsberg, Guy de la Valdene, Russell Chatham, Warren Oates, Jimmy Buffet,

Peter Fonda, and several others.

I once spent the night in Cabin 2, where Brautigan lived while writing *The Hawkline Monster*. Sadly, those cabins are now gone, destroyed by the person who owned this magical place between the great days of Ned and Dan and these new days of Chip and Jen. It's wonderful that these new owners are doing much to make Pine Creek my favorite venue again.

Cabin 2
for Gatz

After the reading
I fill my pockets
with bottles of beer
& follow her
into Cabin 2
where Brautigan
years before, wrote
one of his mad & beautiful
books & where now
for lack of kindling
I throw a copy of my own book
into the wood stove
remembering Buson:

> This cold winter night
> that old wooden-head Buddha
> would make a nice fire

They're both long gone
lost in shadows cast
by the flames of this stove
around which we
drink our beers
& within a few years
this cabin will be
torn down by
some rich asshole

Vagabond Song

> who envisions a future
> free of poets &
> the fires they are always
> starting

#55 – 58: US-89, US-12, MT-200 & MT-3 to Cassiopeia Books

A RETURN TO GREAT FALLS, but this time traveling with my friend, the vagabond musician Greg Klyma. He flew out from Boston for a show at Elk River Books, and from there, we hit the Silver Dollar in Butte and a couple live radio sessions, but for the Cassiopeia gig, I'm his opening act.

Driving up from Livingston and stopping for lunch in White Sulphur Springs, then into the wonder of the Little Belt Mountains. We stop halfway through for a short walk into the slick rocks and fir trees with yellow-bellied marmots zipping over boulders and stumps. Once in Great Falls, we grab a couple drinks at a bar near the bookstore. Another guy there in a fedora compliments mine. Kindred spirits. Comrades in the anti-baseball hat faction.

After the reading and concert, we visit the mermaids at the Sip 'n Dip. And, a first sighting for me, a merman. The sexual revolution is alive and well in Montana.

Extremes

> A slurry of sleet softens to snow
> topping the Little Belts, descending
> to the high plains exhalation
> of Great Falls where
> you trade poems for drinks
> beneath the green flash of mermaids
>
> Late morning & you find yourself
> standing with the longest river

in the country on your left
& the shortest on your right
Stretching you could dip a hand in both

But the sun is on the move &
you still have the long drive home
Back in the parking lot
some guy is telling his son
A carp can grow to six feet long

*At that point he's considered
a man-eater* & you think –
There are a thousand ways to be devoured
You invent new ones every day
Sometimes you're the fish, sometimes the bait
But almost never the one setting the hook

On the way home, we stop off at Bar 47 in White Sulphur. Greg wanders over to the beat-up piano in the corner and starts plinking. Right away, the owner turns off the house music and joins him for a duet of "Crazy." And just like that, I have a new favorite bar.

#59 – 64: I-75, M-33, M-72, M-32, M-68 & M-27 to Purple Tree Books

WE FLY INTO BAY CITY, MICHIGAN – my hometown, though barely recognizably so. All the empty shells of downtown buildings have been given new life with condos and boutiques and antique shops and gourmet this-and-thats. The long abandoned shipworks – gigantic, hulking structures with thousands of broken windows – have been replaced by "Uptown," a shiny cluster of new restaurants, shops and office buildings. In a moment of surrealism, I'm having a chardonnay at a sidewalk bistro with luxury condos above when I realize this used to be the Mill End store with its warped creaking floors and an octogenarian elevator operator who took you to a basement full of wooden bins of hardware, fishing lures, penny toys and army surplus gear, or upstairs to find bolts of plain, durable fabric, cast iron frying pans and winter coats.

Sometimes the more that things change, they more they change.

We drive up M-33 into the heart of northern Michigan, "Up North" as we say around here. It's a reunion with many old and dear friends: quaking aspen and paper birch, staghorn sumac and bracken fern, jack pine and white cedar. I've made some new floral friends in my years in Montana, hiking the Absarokas and floating the Yellowstone, but none have become as close as these Northwoods companions and comrades. Every type of tree or shrub or wildflower here flushes a covey of memories.

After a fantastic lunch at a diner in Onaway, we buy a homemade rhubarb pie and finish the drive to a rental cabin on Lake Huron, almost at the very Tip of the Mitt (an expression that makes perfect sense to Michiganders). Directly across from our 20 feet of beach, Bois Blanc Island spreads out across the horizon. A magical place that I visit in *Vagabond Song*:

> Beneath the Wild Rice Moon
> Drunk & dancing with bats
> on Bois Blanc Island
> a bottle in one hand
> a million stars in the other ...

These waters of the Straits of Mackinac are among the most beautiful and magical I've known. And of course, like everything of beauty and magic in this world, they are threatened by short-sighted greed. Enbridge's Line 5 pipelines, built in 1953, carry nearly 23 million gallons of oil and natural gas per day across the Straits – the heart of 20% of the freshwater on earth. The pipes show structural damage that Enbridge lies about or dismisses. This is the same company that caused the largest inland oil spill in U.S. history, in the Kalamazoo River, then ignored it for seventeen hours. No amount of profit, or any other perceived benefit, is worth risking the northern Great Lakes.

My reading at Purple Tree Books starts out slow. Slow as in, no one there. I don't blame anyone for not wanting to be indoors on the first day of the holiday weekend. But a few people eventually trickle in, and we sit around a table and have a great chat. I read a handful of new poems and an excerpt from *Vagabond Song*. We trade road trip stories and memories of shared places. As almost always happens with a small turn-out, it ends up being one of the best. Intimate and filled with good new connections. The kind of reading where I can thank each person by name. (Thanks Emily, Christine, Leea, Lisa and Mom!) And really, that's the kind of thing that makes a book tour memorable and this whole writing game worth it.

#65, 66: US-23 & I-75 to Bayliss Public Library

BEING FROM THE LOWER PENINSULA OF MICHIGAN, the U.P. feels like having a mystical, ghost-like sibling. Yes, we're related, but something magical and unknown is going on up there. We trolls (who live below the bridge) can visit, we can make jokes about Yoopers, but the land and waters of the Upper Peninsula will always enchant us.

Driving into Sault Ste. Marie, where I have a reading booked at the local library, I almost crash when I see my name flashing

Vagabond Song

on a big sign above the bridge entering downtown. I'm used to seeing my name in plastic on a bar marquee or chalk on a coffeehouse sidewalk sign, but dogdamn this is the first time seeing my name in lights. What a great welcome!

Sault Ste. Marie was known as *Bawating*, "The Gathering Place," by its Anishinaabe inhabitants, and gather we do. The room is packed, the readers for the open mic are passionate, and the Q&A is as lively as they come.

My favorite question, which I don't answer very well, is about my revision process. I get too bogged down in the logistics of revision instead of going into purpose.

It's about listening to the internal music of the poem, and trusting that by following this music, the poem will say what it needs to say. *Re-vise*, "to see again." To get back to the original vision of the piece, before our monkey-mind jumped in with its cleverness or its properness or its logical, respectable editorial hammer. But *re-listen* is a better term. The truth of the poem is in its music. Every line must sing. How? Who the hell knows? There is no formula, no rule book. It's about developing the ear the same way a musician does: Listen. Read hundreds of great poems out loud. Read your own poems out loud hundreds of times. Listen.

#67 – 76: H-58, M-28, M-94, US-2, US-23, M-13, M-247, M-84, M-81 & M-46 to the Theordore Roethke House

AFTER A FEW DAYS ON THE STORMY SHORES of Lake Superior, we drop down to one of my favorite bodies of water in the world: the northern reaches of Lake Michigan. In *Vagabond Song*, I describe it as, "crystalline, memory-cleansing, defying the existence of Gary and Chicago at its other end … this northern dream-bringer …" Despite the chilly day and cold water, we pull off of Highway 2, scramble down to the beach and plunge in. It's my kind of baptism, and always has the effect of renewal, reawakening, reconnection with beauty and life. *Miigwetch, Ininwewi-gichigami.*

Downstate for my reading at the Theodore Roethke Home Museum. When I lived in Saginaw, I had keys to Roethke's childhood home. The folks who ran the house said, "We like the idea of a poet hanging out here, writing poetry." I spent many great nights with fellow Saginista poet Al Hellus, enjoying a jug of cheap wine, trading poems, scribbling in our journals and conjuring rows of greenhouses, long gone, in the dining room window's reflection. It was during one of these sessions that Al and I came up with the idea to co-write a chapbook of our Saginaw-rooted poems. We called it *Saginaw Songs* after Roethke's poem "Saginaw Song." It's a purposefully silly poem, no "Far Field" (a favorite of mine and Al's), but we often quoted it's most fitting line:

> In Saginaw, in Saginaw,
> Bartenders think no ill;
> But they've ways of indicating when
> You are not acting well:
> They throw you through the front plate glass
> And then send you the bill.

The story is that this is a reference to the bar at the Schuch Hotel where Ted took Dylan Thomas during his visit to Saginaw. Who knows if that's true or not, but that place has a long history of drunk poets misbehaving. (No comment.)

Vagabond Song

#77 – 95: I-95, I-76, NJ-42, NJ-41, NJ-47, CR-658, CR-655, CR-634, CR-654, CR-555, CR-557, NJ-40, NJ-50, US-9, NJ-109, CR-606, CR-626, DE-162 & DE-1 to
Rehoboth Beach Public Library

WE DROP INTO THE PHILLY AIRPORT around sunset and muck through a Kafkaesque car rental process – walking through a maze of corridors, missing buses, waiting in a long line only to find out it's the wrong line – until finally, blasting out into traffic and heading across the Walt Whitman bridge into New Jersey. It's perfect that the 100 Highways Tour includes this crossing. Uncle Walt, who I quote near the end of *Vagabond Song*: "Bearded, sunburnt, gray-neck'd, forbidding, I have arrived."

It becomes a long, meandering drive through Jersey, mostly because, in an attempt to avoid toll roads, we become quickly, blissfully lost. We're heading mostly south and will eventually stumble onto a major highway that will zip us to our destination, so for now, we just enjoy the ride.

In my youth, this was always my goal in the Northwoods of Michigan: the moment I realized I didn't know where I was, everything became stunningly beautiful and fraught with possibility. Every moment was savored. I could enjoy the fantasy of simply not returning to the world of concrete and schedules. I could be a hermit, a Han Shan-esque wanderer, a *feralite*.

We have a decent dinner and a few drinks at a friendly roadhouse that appears out of the gloom like a dream, then an hour or two later, fall into the flow of US-9, down into Cape May. We check into a motel then run across the road, ignore the "Beach Closed" signs and stand at the crashing edge of the Atlantic, still surly and fierce from the recent hurricanes. It's humbling to be in proximity to such power. It's good to be humbled by the natural world.

Much of our problems and threats to survival we face stem from a severe lack of this type of humility.

The next day, we hike around some coastal wetlands, glassing birds and learning the names of unfamiliar plants, before jumping the ferry across Delaware Bay into Lewes, the first city in what became the first state. I find a great little bookstore, Biblion, and its friendly owner, Jen. We talk books and the book trade for quite a while, and then I ask her if she has anything on James Joyce. She sells me a great copy of *Coping with Joyce: Essays from the Copenhagen Symposium*, but it's the stuff that isn't for sale that's really exciting: a photo of a manuscript page with notations from the "Cyclops" episode of *Ulysses*, the original discovered locally, and a large format duplicate of the photo of Joyce and Sylvia Beach hanging at her Shakespeare & Co. bookshop in Paris.

It's a fantastic visit that makes me wish that I had booked my reading here.

The actual reading is a total bust. The staff either have no idea that an event had been scheduled or just don't care. I ask if they are going to set up some seating, and get the rude-toned reply, "You can move chairs around if you want, but you have to put them back when you're done." There's been zero promo, so the only crowd is the people I brought with me, and two people who happen to be in the seating area – but they decide to talk over me during the attempted reading. Usually I can win people over and they end up enjoying the event, but the fabled East Coast attitude is strong with these two. They express their annoyance, keep talking, and do their best to deserve a book upside the head.

I cut things short, and head out to find a bar. After, of course, putting the chairs back properly.

Despite that, the overall trip is great, especially a bike ride/bird-watching excursion through Cape Henlopen State Park, the delicious seafood, meeting up with a cousin and her daughter at a great little Mexican cantina near the beach, spending time with Lisa's family, the songs of crickets and mockingbirds, the beer tasting at Dogfish Head Brewery, and on the way back to the airport, a few days wandering the streets of Philly – with its murals and history and live jazz at a great little whiskey bar – and spending long, energizing moments in the humbling beauty of that surly and fierce Mama Ocean.

#96 – 100: CA-87, CA-85, US-101, CA-156 & CA-1 to a cliff overlooking the Pacific

WHAT BETTER PLACE TO END THE TOUR for *Vagabond Song* than on the same road where the book ends: the Pacific Coast Highway on the very farthest edge of that myth we call America? And what better audience than the ocean herself?

We fly into San Jose, grab a rental car and head south to Pacific Grove and our postage stamp hotel room with a view of Monterey Bay and a daily alarm clock of the loudest gulls I've met. This is our base of operations for day trips down the coast, hiking in the redwoods, wandering cliff-fringed beaches and making a pilgrimage to the Henry Miller Memorial Library.

An enchanted courtyard filled with art and trees, a room filled with great books, free tea and the best motto imaginable: "The Henry Miller Memorial Library, where nothing happens." Miller is one of those writers I read too long ago and need to revisit. I vaguely recall *Tropic of Cancer* changing my conception of what a book could be, in the same way that *Ulysses* and *100 Years of Solitude* did.

The Hundred Highways Tour

Eventually, we find the right cliff along the right stretch of the Pacific Coast Highway. I read the final scene from *Vagabond Song* that takes place during a hitchhiking trip down this very road. The plan was to give people a heads up that I was going to broadcast the reading online so they could tune in, but suddenly, we are at the right spot. We don't know if we have an internet connection or not, but we start broadcasting the reading anyway. The result is shaky and marred (or enhanced) by the noise of passing cars, the clip gets cut off right before the final word, and only a handful of people catch it live. But that's okay. The point is to read to the ocean. The point is to celebrate the completion of the Hundred Highways Tour on the same highway as the book's final movement. The point is to toss out these words to the sea and let them fly away like the gulls and cormorants who are with us continuously on this final trip.

It's been a fantastic voyage hitting these hundred highways, meeting great people and sharing my work with them. With you. Thanks for riding shotgun. May your roads be winding, wild and filled with music. May you meet many Vagabond Angels, and may you be one to others.

See you on the next hundred.

~M

On the 100 Highways Tour, at the Continental Divide
Photo by Lisa Snow

Marc Beaudin is a poet, theatre artist and bookseller in Livingston, Montana. In addition to his books, he has released two albums of spoken word and jazz featuring music by members of the band Morphine and the Northwoods Improvisers. He still believes the Brahms' *Violin Concerto in D* is more powerful than all the guns, smokestacks and authoritarians in the world.

Edd Enders was born in Livingston and studied art at Montana State University. He has worked on archeological survey teams throughout the West, and as a hunting guide, packer, wrangler and cowboy from Alaska to Arizona. His work has collectors from New York to Key West to Chicago to Shanghai, and has been shown in numerous solo and group exhibitions.

William Heyen is a National Book Award finalist, a Fulbright Lecturer and a recipient of awards from the NEA, the Guggenheim Foundation and the American Academy of Arts & Letters. He has published nearly 50 books of poetry, memoir and essay, and has appeared in hundreds of journals. His collection of scherzi, *Timewarp & Numbnuts*, is forthcoming from Elk River Books.

Sources

M-72
p. 4: "All mine Oten reedes …" Edmund Spenser, *The Shepheards Calender* (Cambridge: Cambridge UP, 1923).
p. 5: "God is terse. …" "I poke my stick …" Jim Harrison, *After Ikkyū and Other Poems* (Boston: Shambhala, 1996).
p. 8: "When I breathe with the birds …" Theodore Roethke, "Journey to the Interior" *Collected Poems* (Garden City: Doubleday, 1966).

Trail Ridge & West Elk Loop
p. 15: "I love you baby but you got to understand …" Hank Williams, "Ramblin' Man" (MGM Records, 1953).
p. 15: "You're gonna cry 96 tears." Rudy Martinez, "96 Tears" (Cameo-Parkway, 1966).
p. 17: "You have loved forty women …" Carl Sandburg, "Personality" *Chicago Poems* (New York: Henry Holt, 1916).
p. 17: "Don't the highway look lonesome …" Muddy Waters, "Thirteen Highway" (MCA/Chess, 1994).
p. 20: "We live as we dream, alone." Joseph Conrad, *Heart of Darkness* (New York: Norton, 1988).
p. 23: "Travel is fatal to prejudice …" Mark Twain, *Innocents Abroad* (Oxford: Oxford UP, 1996).
p. 27: "I am Vasuki …" Swami Prabhavananda and Christopher Isherwood, trans., *Bhagavad-Gita* (New York: Signet, 1954).
p. 28: "*Nanisana, nanisana …*" quoted in James Mooney, *The Ghost Dance Religion and the Sioux Outbreak of 1890* (Chicago: U of Chicago P, 1965).
p. 31: "Corn grew where the corn was spilled …" Thomas Hornsby Ferril, "No Mark" *Trial by Time* (New York: Harper, 1944).
p. 36: "Do not lay up for yourselves treasures on earth …" Matthew 6:19-21; "If you would be perfect …" Matthew 19:21, *The Bible, Revised Standard Version* (Teaneck: Cokesbury, 1971).
p. 36: "We're chained to the world …" Tom Waits, "Dirt in the Ground" *Bone Machine* (Island Records, 1992).
p. 37: "Not through much learning …" Juan Mascaró, ed. "Katha Upanishad," *The Upanishads* (New York: Penguin, 1965).
p. 43: "Now the music volleys through …" William Carlos Williams, "The Desert Music" *The Collected Poems, Vol. 2*

(New York: New Directions, 1991).
p. 48: "Go to sleep you weary hobo ..." Goebel Reeves, "Hobo's Lullaby."
p. 50: "At the risk of seeming ridiculous ..." Che Guevara, "Man and Socialism in Cuba" *The Che Reader* (Minneapolis: Ocean Press, 2005).
p. 52: "Shake the ground with the night-long dances ..." Sophocles, "Antigone" *The Theban Plays* (New York: Penguin, 1974).

State Road 107 & the Music Highway
p. 64: "I don't know just where I'm going ..." Lou Reed, "Heroin" *The Velvet Underground & Nico* (Verve, 1967).
p. 68: "Six miles from earth ..." Randall Jarrell, "Death of the Ball Turret Gunner" *Norton Anthology of Modern Poetry* (New York: Norton, 1973).
p. 69: "May this fire in my soul ..." Johnny Ace, "Pledging My Love" (Duke, 1955).
p. 69: "Your easy rider's gone ..." W.C. Handy, "Yellow Dog Blues" (Victor, 1919).
p. 69: "I want to go home ..." B. B. King, "Bad Luck Soul" (Kent, 1961).
p. 69: "It's 2000 miles I've roamed ..." Otis Redding, "Sitting on the Dock of the Bay" (Stax, 1968).
p. 69: "When I first thought to hoboin'..." John Lee Hooker, "Hobo Blues" (Modern, 1948).
p. 69: "Feel like a broken spoke ..." Memphis Slim, "Blue and Disgusted" *Memphis Slim U.S.A.* (Candid, 1961).
p. 69: "The way is dark ..." Jerry Lee Lewis, "End of the Road" (Sun, 1956).
p. 69: "Somebody done hoodooed the hoodoo man" Junior Wells, "Hoodoo Man Blues" (States, 1953).
p. 69: "Ain't got time to take a fast train ..." The Box Tops, "The Letter" (Mala, 1967).
p. 70: "Boss Crump don't 'low no easy riders ..." W.C. Handy, "Memphis Blues" (Victor, 1914).
p. 70: "More road ahead, but the breath is gone ..." Kabir, *The Bījak of Kabir*, trans. by Linda Hess and Shukdev Singh (Delhi: Motilal, 1986).
p. 77: "[Rudy]: He knew where the Milky Way was." William Kennedy, *Ironweed* (New York: Penguin, 1984).

M-46
p. 85 "technology leader in industrial ..." http://velsicol.com.
p. 85: "I'm naked in soul ..." Al Hellus, "This Thing About Time" *How Much of Your Heart Is Left?* (Roseville: Ridgeway Press, 2008).

The Chicken Bus Highway, Part I
p. 98: "I'm a nomad ..." Faruq Z. Bey, "Spooking in Tongues" *Hymnbook of the Anciency* (Entropy Stereo, 2006).
p. 98: *"Tal vez busca su destino ..."* Octavio Paz, *El laberinto de la soledad y otros obras* (New York: Penguin, 1997).
p. 115: "The point of the journey ..." Neil Peart, "Prime Mover" *Hold Your Fire* (Polygram/Mercury, 1987).

The Chicken Bus Highway, Part II
p. 123: "Everything is holy ..." Allen Ginsburg, *Howl* (San Francisco: City Lights, 1956).
p. 141: *"Non qui parum habet ..."* Lucius Annaeus Seneca; Richard Mott Gummere, trans. *Epistulae morales ad Lucilium* (London: Loeb, 1917).

A1 & The Wicklow Way
p. 158: "We traveled, with hope ..." Roethke, "The Harsh Country" *Collected Poems*.
p. 159: "A tourist doesn't know ..." Paul Theroux, *Happy Isles of Oceania* (New York: Putman, 1992).
p. 168: "Here today, up and off to somewhere else tomorrow ..." Kenneth Grahame, *The Wind in the Willows* (London: Methuen, 1908).
p. 168: "foaming ebon ale ..." James Joyce, *Ulysses* (New York: Random House, 1934).
p. 169: "I was blue moldy for the want of that pint ..." ibid.
p. 170: "babadalghara– ..." Joyce, *Finnegans Wake* (New York: Viking, 1939).
p. 170: "yes I said yes ..." "smiledyawnednodded all in one ..." "two fellows who would suck whiskey ..." Joyce, *Ulysses*.
p. 171: "Every moment of inspiration ..." Joyce, *A Portrait of the Artist as a Young Man* (New York: Viking, 1965).
p. 171: "There is an art, Mr Dedalus ..." Joyce, *Stephen Hero* (London: Jonathan Cape, 1944).

p. 174: "Blow winds and crack your cheeks …" William Shakespeare, *King Lear* (New York: Pelican, 1970).

p. 175: "There's moonlight in the woodpulp …" Hellus, "First Love Comix" *How Much of Your Heart Is Left?*

p. 175: "When the sun goes down …" Hellus, private letter.

Highway 2

p. 191: "I should be paid for discovering …" Antler, *Factory* (San Francisco: City Lights, 1980).

p. 194: "Sun comes up, sun goes down" John Francis Bueche, "Seward Cafe" (unpublished song).

Flying Cloud to the Warrior Trail

p. 202: "Never be deceived that the rich …" Lucy Parsons, *Freedom, Equality & Solidarity: Writings & Speeches, 1878-1937* (Chicago: Charles H. Kerr, 2004).

p. 207: "Life isn't allowed on the Interstates …" William Least Heat-Moon, *Blue Highways* (New York: Ballantine, 1984).

p. 217: "lay waste all the settlements around …" etc. quoted in Ward Churchill, *A Little Matter of Genocide* (San Francisco: City Lights, 1997).

p. 223: "It's a poet's job …" Michael Earl Craig, "Bluebirds" *Thin Kimono* (Seattle: Wave Books, 2010).

p. 223: "Bearded, sun-burnt, …" Walt Whitman, "Starting from Paumanok" *Leaves of Grass* (New York: Signet, 1958).

Coastal Highway

p. 228: "form propped motionless …" William Carlos Williams, "The Desert Music" *Collected Poems, Vol. 2.*

p. 228: "Peculiar travel suggestions …" Kurt Vonnegut, *Cat's Cradle.* (New York: Delacorte Press, 1963).

p. 229: "A poem is a mirror …" Lawrence Ferlinghetti, *Pictures of a Gone World* (San Francisco: City Lights, 1955).

Coda

p. 243: "The best wisdom comes directly …" Doug Peacock, *Walking It Off* (Spokane: Eastern Washington UP, 2005).

Other Titles from
Elk River Books

Unearthing Paradise:
Montana Writers in Defense of Greater Yellowstone
Edited by Max Hjortsberg, Seabring Davis & Marc Beaudin

"A treasure trove of courage and heart
by the blessed rabble." –David James Duncan

The Bluebird Run
Poetry by Greg Keeler

"A true poet of rivers and all the lonely roads to get to them, Keeler seems alone and far away and yet his voice is always, always right there." –Rick Ardinger

Westward & Miserable
Paintings and writings by John Henry Haseltine

"An irreverent rollick, dismantling myths and Gonzoing Western history. Haseltine illustrates his outrageous collection of tall tales and spirited yarns with originality, charm and joyfulness." –Betsy Gaines Quammen

Forthcoming:

Jim Harrison: A Bibliographical Addenda, 2009 - 2025
by Gregg Orr

Timewarp & Numbnuts: The Dials
Poetry by William Heyen

Ordering information at:
ElkRiverBooks.com/press

www.ingramcontent.com/pod-product-compliance
Lightning Source LLC
Chambersburg PA
CBHW062108290426
44110CB00023B/2748